T0283128

CRITICAL PRAISE FOR ALEX WHEATLE'S NOVELS

"Alex Wheatle writes from a place of honesty and passion, with the full knowledge and understanding that change can only happen through words and actions."
—Steve McQueen, Academy Award–winning film director

for *Kemosha of the Caribbean*

• A Junior Library Guild Gold Standard Selection

"A stunning historical adventure that upends stereotypes."
—*Times* (UK)

"Kemosha's indomitable spirit, determination, and wit make for an unforgettable heroine." —*Guardian* (UK)

"Inspired by accounts of women pirates, this fantastical tale represents the era's cruelty without romanticizing it. Kemosha's love and persistence combine with forceful action, the terror of harsh racism, and passionate, colorful language." —*Toronto Star*

"Kemosha's heart and tenacity are endearing." —*Kirkus Reviews*

"Wheatle's swashbuckling latest blends adventure, history, and poignancy ... Well written and full of thrills, this cross between Margarita Engle's *Hurricane Dancers* and L.A. Meyer's Bloody Jack Adventures series will inspire hope and spark admiration." —*Booklist*

"*Kemosha of the Caribbean* is easily the best pirate tale I have ever encountered. If that seems a bold statement, its boldness pales in comparison to Kemosha's enduring bravery and steadfastness."
—*The Plot Thickens*

"Readers are in for a wild ride through this rich mix of cultures, lifestyles, [and] languages." —*Children's Literature*

for *Cane Warriors*r

"Alex Wheatle departs from his award-winning contemporary novels for a superb foray into historical fiction ... Wheatle's characteristic kennings and coinages ... heighten this intense, affecting story of courage, bloodshed, and commitment to freedom at all costs."—*Guardian* (UK)

"I read it in one sitting. I simply could not put it down. *Cane Warriors* is such a powerful narrative of trauma and triumph . . . Wheatle celebrates the heroism that Tacky inspires. He tells the riveting story of fourteen-year-old Moa who bravely joins Tacky's army."

—*Gleaner* (Jamaica)

"Wheatle brings the struggle of slavery in the Jamaican sugarcane fields to life . . . A refreshing and heartbreaking story that depicts both a real-life uprising against oppression and the innate desire to be free. Highly recommended." —*School Library Journal*, starred review

for *Home Girl*

"Another powerful and poignant novel deftly created by one of the most prolific master novelists on either side of the pond. *Home Girl* is a page-turner, with not a dull moment. Loved it from the rooter to the tooter." —Eric Jerome Dickey, author of *Before We Were Wicked*

"Teenager Naomi, old before her time and as vulnerable as she is fierce, is growing up in the care system. Foster homes and pupil referral units reveal the unsettling, often bewildering reality of this existence. Wheatle's empathy, authentic characters, and rich dialogue illuminate the dark." —*Observer Magazine* (UK)

"Naomi Brisset is a teenage girl growing up too fast in the UK care system. Her journey through a series of foster homes exposes the unsettling, often heartwrenching truth of this life. Yet despite the grit, Wheatle's writing is as rich and warm as ever, bringing courage and hope to an unforgettable heroine's story."

—*Bookseller* (UK), Editors' Choice

"With a tough exterior and brash attitude, Naomi is an authentic character in an unfortunate yet accurate picture of modern-day foster care in the UK . . . The ending is neither predictable nor sugarcoated, leaving readers rooting for this determined heroine."

—*School Library Journal*

SUFFERAH
THE MEMOIR OF A BRIXTON REGGAE-HEAD

BY ALEX WHEATLE

Akashic Books
Brooklyn, NY

Published by Akashic Books
©2023 Alex Wheatle

ISBN: 978-1-63614-093-3
Library of Congress Control Number: 2022947076
All rights reserved
First printing

Photos courtesy of Alex Wheatle

Akashic Books
Brooklyn, New York
Instagram, Twitter, Facebook: AkashicBooks
E-mail: info@akashicbooks.com
Website: www.akashicbooks.com

TABLE OF CONTENTS

INTRODUCTION

by Vanessa Walters

Wi liccle but wi tallawah. Small but mighty.

Bob Marley described Jamaica as "the university of the world," and it is nearly impossible to overestimate the global impact of this small island of fewer than three million people. Jamaica has been a pivotal part of world history, from the arrival of Christopher Columbus in 1494, through the genocide and enslavement of the indigenous population and Africans who followed. The lessons of Jamaica's history are humanity's inheritance. Reggae music is part of its distinctive culture that encompasses the political and the existential, influencing protest movements, language evolution, and social transformation worldwide. Within its panoply of forms, the central message remains mental emancipation for the poor, the oppressed, the underestimated.

Sufferah, if they can but recognize their own innate power.

The sufferah takes center stage in many of Alex Wheatle's stories. From Brenton Brown, the troubled mixed-race youth abandoned in the foster care system, to enslaved Kemosha, who becomes a swashbuckling pirate to liberate her people, Alex aptly illustrates the Jamaican proverb. The small but mighty hero or antihero takes on a hostile environment, often at a terrible personal cost, for a purpose bigger than themself.

Certain parallels might, I suppose, be drawn between the sufferah and standard-issue superheroes. Like Superman, the sufferah is disadvantaged from birth, sometimes lonely in their predicament, often on the outside looking in longingly, and just as Jor-El tasks his disheartened son with giving the same people who reject him "an ideal to strive toward," the sufferah must also uplift humanity either within the pages or beyond. At least Superman gets to hide who he is behind the socially accepted disguise of Clark Kent. He finds acceptance and safety by cloaking his powers and knowledge with a nonthreatening persona. In contrast, the sufferah, by definition, is seen as antisocial, as unkempt or aggressive, mentally impaired—like the Rastafarians of Jamaica, the original persecuted sufferahs, were judged to be.

At first glance, Alex's sufferahs might seem to challenge the reader to find any empathy for them. For instance, in *East of Acre Lane*, Biscuit is a Brixton drug dealer working for a sadistic gang leader. These sufferahs mostly don't apologize for who they are either—if they even have self-awareness. They kick and scream their way onto the page. Yet we like them immediately, possibly recognizing the part of ourselves that resists conformity, or as one might root for a balloon tossed around in the wind, anxious about where it might end up.

Brenton Brown, Liccle Bit, Moa, Kemosha, Naomi, Biscuit—Alex has found many sufferahs for his award-winning novels. But now he takes us on a very personal sufferah journey: his own.

In the aftermath of slavery in Jamaica, Marcus Garvey is credited with initiating the Black consciousness movement that became central to Jamaican culture. Despite being dismissed by the elite of his time, Garvey was revered by the lower classes as a prophet, giving rise to the Rastafarian movement. The movement rejected the colonial view of Black people as spiritually and physically inferior, instead centering Africa and Black people in conscious thought. Rastafarians survived repeated and often brutal attempts by the Jamaican government to destroy their movement. Eventually, they become known for their dreadlocks, antiestablishment stance, and a heightened sense of self, demonstrated by the unique use of the personal pronoun "I" and other words altered to fit their philosophy.

And then came the reggae: the thunder, lightning, "drum blood story," electric storms, the rhythm of history setting the pace for violent uprising as explained in "Reggae Sounds," a poem by the UK-based Jamaican dub poet and activist Linton Kwesi Johnson. Alex's journey explores how reggae music sustained him through some of the most turbulent moments in his life and how these anthems provided context and companionship in his struggle. It was an unspoken language between others like him, offering a safe space free from hostility. Signposts that gave them a trajectory through the harsh winds of Great Britain. The Windrush immigration era (1948–1971) was sensationalized in Enoch Powell's 1968 "Rivers of Blood" speech. A succession of laws were passed to restrict the flow of nonwhites to the United Kingdom. Ten years after Powell, Prime Minister Margaret Thatcher promoted fears that the UK "might be rather swamped by people with a different culture." At the same time, she positioned the British character as morally superior and implied that xenophobia was justified.

Black people found themselves targeted by the racially applied stop-and-search "SUS" law, under attack from white nationalist groups, and obstructed in their search for employment and accommodation. The suffering was widespread.

Films such as Harold Ové's *Pressure* (1976) described a generation in crisis, and *Babylon* (1980) chronicled the rise of the reggae sound systems against the backdrop of endemic racism. Alex's story is challenging reading at times yet never gets too dark, because we know that our sufferah has made it through. He also finds light even in the darkest of situations and shows us how far a little empathy can take us. How strong the human spirit is.

From Dickensian beginnings, Alex Wheatle has risen to be one of the most lauded writers in Great Britain and beyond, deservedly honored with an MBE for services to literature in 2008. His 2016 book *Crongton Knights* won the fiftieth *Guardian* Children's Fiction Prize, while others have been translated into multiple languages and adapted for theater and television. Alex's remarkable life story is the basis of the fourth film in *Small Axe*, Steve McQueen's critically acclaimed anthology series about the Caribbean community in the UK during the 1970s and '80s.

How on earth did he make it through? It's a question that confronts us often as young Alec Alphonso Wheatle endures shocking abuse in the Shirley Oaks children's home, and Wheatle the teenager runs riot (literally) through the streets of South London. We sit in the prison cell with him, smelling the stench of the shit bucket. We watch him flailing in his proverbial sea of troubles, wondering what fresh hell awaits him next.

But the clue is in the lyrics of the tunes he offers us. Rethinking oneself. The cornerstone instead of the castaway. Love instead of hate. Although riven by loneliness, he found joy and empathy among his reggae greats. These were friends and mentors—who understood what a young Black man was going through, who gave purpose to despair, whether plaintive commiseration or a mischievous croon. Pretty incredible to see every aspect of his life covered in the songs listed.

Whether real or imagined, Alex's stories are a gift to us to never lose hope. His books are loved worldwide for their vivid, relatable characters and heart-pounding scenes. They were inspired by a boy in the UK who knew nothing about himself but found a rich heritage. If Jamaica is the university of the world, Alex Wheatle is its chancellor.

Vanessa Walters

Vanessa Walters, author of *The Nigerwife*, is a novelist, playwright, and journalist originally from London, now based in New York. She is of Jamaican heritage and has written extensively about the British-Caribbean experience. Her published work includes *Smoke! Othello!* and the young adult books *Rude Girls* and *The Best Things in Life*. Her plays have been staged across the UK.

PROLOGUE

....

HM Prison Wormwood Scrubs, June 1981
The stench of excrement filled my nose. Simeon, my Rasta-farian cellmate, had me in a headlock. Tears streamed down my cheeks. I didn't want to be alive. *If there is a God, why is He mocking me?*

I could never get used to the smell, so Dennis Brown sang in "Three Meals a Day."

I gathered in a breath and let loose a primal scream. I tried to rid myself of all the pain, loss, injustice, and bitterness that I carried with me. Simeon placed a hand over my mouth. I tried to bite it. My body convulsed. I once again attempted to wriggle free from his firm hold.

"Calm down, my yout'," Simeon pleaded. "Calm down. Why you try and kill me, eh? You t'ink me so easy to mash up?"

I was exhausted. Physically and mentally. I hyperventilated. Simeon released me. I sat myself against the wall and tried to control my breathing. Simeon looked at me hard. His eyes flicked toward the cell door. Maybe he considered informing the night warden of my mental state.

I'm talkin' about detention, detention, Dennis's voice echoed in my head. *I'm talkin' about detention.*

Simeon took pity on me. He parked himself beside me and his intense gaze never left me alone.

"Someting eating you up, man," he said. "Someting bad."

I didn't respond.

"Tell me your story, Alex," he urged. "*Every mon t'ink his burden is the heaviest*, Bob Marley say. Unpack your burden."

I stared into space, wiped the tears from my face, and turned to him. "No one's ever gave a fuck about me," I snapped. "From the day I was born!"

"Start from the beginning," he said.

"I don't know my beginning. I'm nothing. A nobody."

"That's how the people who are against you want you to feel."

"It's true," I said. "I have nothing. I have nobody."

"Everybody ah somebody," Simeon smiled. "Yes, you have the fierce eyes of ah true-born sufferah. But you t'ink you're the only one who experience nuff tribulation?"

I caught a hint of loss in Simeon's eyes. Maybe some dark memory. He quickly recovered his composure.

"No," I replied.

"Tell me your sufferah's tale," Simeon pressed. "The one ting we do have is time."

I glared at the wall, wanting to headbutt it. I turned to him once more. "Okay," I said.

I didn't count the minutes and hours as I spilled out my life experiences to Simeon during that long night. He listened patiently, sometimes nodding, sometimes caressing his dreadlocks and closing his eyes in meditation.

"Rough inna Babylon," he'd comment. "The devil walks among we. But so does good. Never forget that."

PART 1

YOU CAN'T BLAME THE YOUTH

Here I am in 1963 in the care of Miss Bibsy

AN UNSUITABLE BIRTH

....

I was born Alec Alphonso Wheatle in London on January 3, 1963, into a volatile situation.

My mother, Almira, who had arrived in the UK in the early 1960s without her husband and children, had a brief affair with my Jamaican-born father, Alfred. My mother's husband came over to the UK on a surprise visit in the fall of 1962, only to find his wife pregnant. Almira worried about caring for me because I wasn't her husband's child. She had an impossible choice to make; she feared for my future if she chose to raise me.

Almira came to a decision. She entrusted me to Alfred when I was a few days old before returning to Jamaica where I had five older siblings. I only became aware that I had one brother and four sisters when I read my social services files nineteen years later. To this day, I haven't received any explanation for why the authorities kept this information from me. If I had known, I might not have felt so desperately alone in my formative years.

As a single parent in the mid-1960s, Alfred did the best he could.

I was placed with various babysitters and temporary foster care families while Alfred worked as a carpenter in and around Brixton. He would later tell me about the brutal winter of 1963 when there was still thick snow on the ground in South London in late April. "Me felt so damn cold that me mama feel it in her bones inna Jamaica."

My mother Almira when she was a young woman

When I fell ill with asthma and eczema, it became very complicated to find the necessary care and attention I required. Alfred contacted the Lambeth social services in early 1964. The office was located on Herne Hill Road, just off

Coldharbour Lane in Brixton. It was the street where my mother used to reside—Carnegie Library, a couple minutes' walk up the road, fed her love of reading.

My father in Brixton in the late 1950s

Starting in late January 1964, social services began monitoring me.

In February 1964, my health deteriorated to such an extent that I was admitted to Kings College Hospital in Camberwell and then moved on to Sydenham's Children's Hospital.

On discharge, I was sent to Ladywell Children's Centre, near Lewisham, where they had the facilities to treat my asthma and eczema. Meanwhile, Alfred went to the Jamaican High Commission to see if he could obtain a passport to send me back to his parents in Jamaica.

Social services rejected the proposal, reasoning that they couldn't be assured of my health and safety in Jamaica. My paternal grandparents penned letters asking when their grandson would arrive.

The authorities explained to Alfred that the state could offer me the best care. He believed them.

Years later, friends of my father revealed to me that "Freddie" wanted his old life back: meeting with friends over the weekend, listening to music, clubbing, and drinking pints of Guinness. He also loved to visit South London dog tracks and place a flutter on a greyhound. Fortune didn't bless him.

Eventually, the pressure of caring for me took its toll on Alfred's mental health. Suffering from stress and on the verge of a breakdown, he agreed with social services to place me in permanent care.

In the summer of 1966, I was packed off to the Shirley Oaks children's home, located on the outskirts of the London borough of Croydon. It was situated on the Kent/Surrey border, ten or so miles southeast of Brixton. From that point forward, I had no family contact whatsoever.

I was essentially orphaned.

In the nineteenth century, the seventy-two-acre property was called the Shirley Lodge Farm. The Bermondsey Board of Guardians, searching for a suitable site to house poor children and orphans from the slum spillage of southeast London, bought the land in 1900. They considered it an upgrade from the workhouses depicted in Charles Dickens's *Oliver Twist*. (I used to get up very early on Saturday mornings and watch Charlie Chaplin shorts—I had no idea that he once resided in a workhouse.) They built thirty-eight cottages to accommodate up to sixteen children each.

In the early days of the twentieth century, a children's band from Shirley Oaks regularly marched through central Croydon to raise funds for the home.

London County Council took over the administration of the village in 1930. Children from all over London were sent to the facility, sometimes ripped away from their poverty-stricken parents.

Lambeth Council assumed control of the children's home in 1965.

You entered the institution from the Wickham Road entrance through a gap in the seven-foot perimeter wall. The Shirley Inn public house and a fish-and-chip shop stood opposite. When it was first constructed, there was a front gate where all visitors had to report to the "the lodge" office and be signed in. In later years, anyone could walk through the grounds of Shirley Oaks without being checked or asked for identification.

The village had its own nursery, primary school, and sick bay. A resident doctor and a barber passed through every week. New children were checked for lice and other ailments. There was a maintenance department, engineering depot, cobbler's room, laundry, and small swimming pool, clothing repair, and sewing units all on site. I remember watching Prince Charles's investiture in the Shirley Oaks community center in 1969. There were May Day parades where children wore fancy clothes. Father Christmas did his rounds on Christmas Eve carrying a sackful of chocolate sweets.

We even had our own water tower that dominated the skyline.

There was a children's adventure area where they had constructed a breeze-block castle atop a mud mound. We called this area the "piggery"; arguments, confrontations, and fights were played out here. A World War II jeep and a log square the size of a boxing ring fired the imaginations of many a youngster.

It was managed (not sure if that's the right word) by a superintendent who lived in his own mansion within the grounds, complete with sprawling gardens and water features (his children didn't attend either the nursery or the primary school). When Lambeth Council took over, the superintendent reported to his superiors at Blue Star House, Brixton, the headquarters of the borough's social services.

The physical landscape of Shirley Oaks was stunning; once outside their cottages, children could explore a healthy outdoor lifestyle.

But for so many, the reality of living as a defenseless child in Shirley Oaks was terrifying, deeply traumatic, and life-changing.

As I settled into my new life, Alfred returned to Jamaica without me. He never revealed what my grandparents said to him when they met him at Norman Manley International Airport in Kingston. Nor did he ever return to the UK. He decided to take up teaching and gave lessons on woodworking and technical drawing in a Kingston secondary school.

My mother, who had lost touch with Alfred, had no idea that I was residing in social services care. It was a tragedy for her as much as it was for me.

I was placed in Holly House (every cottage was named after a plant or a tree) where neglect and torture awaited me.

This is me at Holly House, Shirley Oaks

I was very sick in my early years. When I was around six years old, because of my chronic asthma, I was sent to the St. Giles School for "delicate children" on Featherbed Lane, near New Addington (they have since moved to South Croydon). Their main focus was disabled children and young people with mental health issues.

I was picked up in a green bus very early in the morning, and I'd offer to help push the wheelchair-bound children onto the vehicle via a ramp as the driver collected them.

Far away from my living environment, I enjoyed happy

times attending St. Giles where I was encouraged to read, draw, and express myself (I was extremely shy). We'd sing songs together. Cliff Richard's "Congratulations" and the Beatles's "All You Need Is Love" spring to mind.

I raced through the Peter and Jane books, and I was presented with chocolate snacks for my literary skills.

I fondly remember a school trip to the Biggin Hill airbase, which had launched attacks into Nazi Germany during World War II. Standing next to a Spitfire or a Hurricane airplane inspired my ambitions. We all returned to St. Giles dreaming of becoming pilots.

I looked forward to Christmas TV showings of *The Dam Busters* and *633 Squadron* movies.

My only disappointment was being bussed back home to Shirley Oaks every afternoon. Quite often, I lashed out and refused to board the bus. I wanted to live at St. Giles with kind staff looking after me.

The cottages in Shirley Oaks all had outhouses that contained coal and coke bunkers for the dining room, lounge, and boiler fires.

When I was considered big enough (seven years old), I was ordered to fetch the coal—my first chore. The lip of the coal bucket kissed my waist. If I spilled any of the black stuff on the carpet, I was given corporal punishment and worse. Often, the lighting failed in the coal or coke bunker, and I had to scrabble around with my bare hands. I dared not return to the house with a half-empty bucket.

When I reflect on those early years, the Wailers's "Corner Stone" plays in my mind. It's a beautiful Bob Marley original. The reggae legend was abandoned himself by his father as a child. *The stone that the builder refuse will always be the head corner stone.* It's almost as if he wrote the lyrics specifically for me. I guess that's what makes him a genius—I'm sure millions of other fans have a similar reaction.

When I'm feeling down, this is one of the songs I always reach for. It gives me a sense of importance and belonging. Yes, I *am* somebody, despite the rejection I suffered at such a young age.

REGGAE AWAKENING

....

It was fast approaching the hot summer of 1976. My best friend at the time, Valentine Golding, who I met in my first year at secondary school, was always late for his classes. He'd forget his math and history books, homework, and almost everything else. But he'd always remember to bring in his PE kit and his tape recorder/player. The keys to operate the machine were almost the same size as a piano's. He'd bring in TDK cassette tapes (it had to be TDK for the best quality sound).

Valentine had a brother-in-law who he called Papa Cass who was a master carpenter. He also owned the Arrows sound system, a turntable and a multispeaker box unit that played reggae music in halls, clubs, and house parties. He built all the equipment himself.

When Valentine was meant to be studying and reviewing the events that led to Anne Boleyn's beheading or working out an algebra formula, he was hanging around Papa Cass's listening to and recording reggae music.

One warm June morning while Valentine and I sat in history class, he simply couldn't wait for the lunch bell. He couldn't stop grinning. During the lesson, he pressed a button on his cassette player and released the tones of Rupie Edwards's "Irie Feelings." I had never heard anything quite like it. Even on Valentine's low-wattage machine, we could feel the bass. The echo and reverb on the track were hypnotic. He pressed rewind. The white kids sitting around us didn't know what to make of it. They stared at each other. One of them took offense and made references to "jungle music." The teacher looked like he had just encountered a yeti before he composed himself and warned Valentine, "Turn that bloody thing off."

Valentine had to be asked six times before he finally obliged.

"What is it?" I asked Valentine.

"Reggae," he replied. "Skanga, skanga, skanga!"

"It's jungle music!" repeated the white boy. "Why don't you two fuck off back to the jungle with it?"

It didn't take much to provoke a reaction from me when I heard racist abuse. I managed to get in a few uppercuts and right crosses before teachers intervened and I was dragged away.

As far back as I can remember, I was made to feel inferior because of the color of my skin. I cannot pinpoint the first time I was subjected to racist abuse. It was simply a part of my lived experience as a child. Popular television sitcoms of the day like *Love Thy Neighbour* and successful comedians such as Jim Davidson and Bernard Manning only intensified my sense that I was lesser than white people.

My violent reaction to racial taunting was a recurring cycle in 1976 and 1977. I was suspended four times and expelled twice. Teachers forever counseled me to ignore the taunts and allow them to deal with any name-calling incidents. "Sticks and stones may break your bones but words should never hurt you," they repeated.

Various social workers and authorities at Shirley Oaks struggled to convince other schools in the Croydon borough to accept me. They hosted case review meetings to discuss "Alex Wheatle's violent episodes," but they never considered why I carried such fury. They simply labeled me maladjusted. I had no idea what that meant or how it was spelled.

Before my final expulsion, staff at the reform school I attended forced me into a straitjacket and left me on the gym floor for the whole afternoon.

I lay perfectly still on the floor, not quite believing how my world hated me so much.

Strangely enough, I enjoyed school. History and PE were my favorite subjects. I always made it onto the football, basketball, and cricket teams and barely anybody could better me in a spelling test.

I'm not sure if I had ever heard a reggae track before Valentine brought in his cassette player. "Irie Feelings" is the first one I can remember. It didn't sound like anything they had on *Top of the Pops*. At thirteen, my favorite bands included Tavares, the Drifters, the Stylistics, the Real Thing, and almost any other soul or disco outfit. I loved Stevie Wonder too.

Reggae hooked me from the start. It's been a love affair that has never let me down.

During the 1976 heat wave, Papa Cass taught Valentine the art of building sound system speaker boxes. Valentine once brought me around to Papa Cass's garden shed where he kept his midrange speakers. I thought my eyes betrayed me when I spotted a one-armed bandit gambling machine that had been hollowed out and converted into a metal speaker box.

I'll never forget Valentine's smile as he watched me admiring Papa Cass's creativity.

"One day we'll have our own sound system," Valentine promised.

"How are we gonna do that?" I asked.

"We'll find a way," he told me.

The summer of 1976 was one of the hottest on record. Reservoirs dried up, parks turned brown, ice cream vans made a killing, and Black groups started to appear on *Top of the Pops*. For most of my free time I walked around in a pair of red Adidas shorts that I had shoplifted from the Allders department store in central Croydon (security spotted me but couldn't catch me). One girl at school said I had nice strong legs, so I thought I'd show them off.

The fashion of the day for teenage boys was flared, high-waisted trousers, platform shoes, fly shirts where the tips of the collar kissed your shoulders, and a gold chain to sex up your neck if you could afford it. The girls in my year had grown tired of the Bay City Rollers tartan look. They boasted two-tone skirts, Crimplene blouses, and thin gold necklaces. This was all before 1977's John Travolta and *Saturday Night Fever* swept the world.

I didn't own even half of the above. In my situation, I was lucky to own a pair of slacks from C&A. Yet I was still determined to try out a new dance move or three at the YMCA disco in East Croydon. They held it every Friday evening.

With my saved-up paper-round money, and my Michael Jackson Afro that I had been flicking and caressing into shape for the best part of an hour, I would jump on a 119, 166, or 194 bus from Shirley to East Croydon. Excitement danced through my veins. I even practiced my new moves on the top deck. I had perfected my line-dance steps to Rose Royce's "Car Wash."

At the disco, I boogied to Tavares, the Stylistics, Barry White, Earth, Wind & Fire, Wild Cherry, James Brown, Van McCoy, and many more. It was all very good—but Valentine and I wanted to hear some reggae music!

We hollered at the DJ and implored him, as Valentine would put it, to play "ah liccle drum and bass."

The only reggae record the white DJ owned was Junior Murvin's "Police & Thieves." When he placed the needle on the vinyl and *that* bass dropped, the crowd went nuts. Suddenly, all the reggae-heads, who may have been hanging in the lobby or smoking spliffs outside, raced inside. "Rewind! Rewind! Rewind!" they chanted. *Police and thieves in the street . . .*

The falsetto vocal, riding over a murderous bass line and echoing guitar, was simply pure genius. What Lee "Scratch" Perry produced in his sparsely equipped, cramped studio in Jamaica was mind-boggling.

We reggae-heads would have to wait until the end of the dance for our moment, but when it arrived, we celebrated like we were jamming at Notting Hill Carnival.

From the YMCA disco, we would strut to the newly opened McDonald's on Croydon High Street. To save face, I often spent my bus fare on a cheeseburger, fries, and a chocolate milkshake and walked home.

I had no funds left for the nearby late-night cinema that screened Hong Kong kung fu movies like *Snake & Crane Arts of Shaolin*, *Snake in the Eagle's Shadow*, and *The Victim*. But this didn't stop me from practicing my flying kicks halfway between Shirley and East Croydon.

POST-CURFEW SKANKING

· ·

I was introduced to the Parchmore Youth Club in Thornton Heath by my Shirley Oaks sisters Denise and Brenda in the fall of 1976. I was thirteen and knew little of the world outside of the home. I had played for the school football team on fields in New Addington, Mitcham, Merton, Sutton, South Norwood, and Thornton Heath, but I had never roamed at night in those locales.

The heat wave had ended, homeowners could water their gardens once more, and kids who played truant at the open-air swimming pool by Purley Way found other locations in which to hide from school.

Parchmore Youth Club had the usual fare: pool table, table football, banter, a resident boom-box guy, an arts-and-crafts space, and a TV room. It also had a once-a-fortnight event that no other youth club that I knew of could ever match: a sound system dance. When I heard this news, I almost combusted with excitement and anticipation.

My curfew at the children's home was still nine p.m. The dance finished at ten p.m. *A live sound system!* I simply had to attend.

Brenda, Denise, and I took the 194b bus from Shirley to Thornton Heath. The youth club was a five-minute step from the clock tower. Denise had already advised me to "burn" my flared pants, fly shirt, and school shoes. "You can't go in there looking like a soul boy! Don't shame us!"

I wore my black school trousers, a blue T-shirt, and borrowed a pair of black moccasins that were too tight. Again, I didn't care that my toes were crushed—I just *had* to be there.

Once we arrived, I felt an unbelievable sense of belonging. It was much darker than any disco I had ever attended. The only light I could see was the red one glowing from the sound system's control tower. I noticed it wasn't just cigarettes the ravers were smoking. It was a joy to be surrounded by other reggae-heads.

The resident sound system was the Mighty Observer, operated by a dreadlocked guy named Austin. One of his crew was a bulky brother nicknamed Rhino. When he hit the floor, you had to be careful he didn't take you out with his wild skanking, hence his moniker.

The first track Austin played as I took up my position close to a double-bass speaker box was the Heptones's "Party Time."

Although this version of the song wasn't the original, it could not have been produced by anyone else but the great Lee "Scratch" Perry. Four seconds into the track, I knew it was him. The positive lyrics bounced along to a superb rhythm track that got me moving immediately. *You've got to live some life . . .* It had the trademark Scratch echo and reverb underscored by a rolling bass line. I put my ear close to the eighteen-inch bass speaker and I swear it cooled off the sweat on my forehead. Like most Scratch productions, it has a timeless quality to it.

The lead singer and songwriter was the unheralded Leroy Sibbles. For me, he is an absolute giant of reggae music, one of the artists who created the genre. While working for Cox-sone Dodd's Studio One label as a bassist, songwriter, and arranger, he laid down rhythms and bass lines that are still being sampled and used today.

I arrived home just after eleven p.m. I was screamed at, threatened with being grounded, and warned how dangerous it was to walk the streets late at night.

Ironic. The most danger I had ever been exposed to was in Holly House.

They could no longer physically abuse me or intimidate me. By the time I had reached twelve, I'd started fighting back with fists, shoes, and on one occasion, a coal shovel I picked up to defend myself.

In another incident, I smashed my housemother Joyce Cook's glasses, right-hooked her jaw, and kicked her on the ground. Other staff pulled me off her, dragged me outside, and locked me in the outhouse to cool off.

Lurking in the corner of the outhouse was what looked like the remains of some sort of scarecrow. Years later, I de-scribed this scenario in my novel *Brixton Rock*.

Still, "Party Time" and so many other new reggae songs I first heard that night in Parchmore made my confinement more than tolerable.

EXTRACTING MAXIMUM BASS

······························

By early 1977, I had made a new friend in the Shirley Oaks children's home village: a boy named Dwight Grant. He was two years older than me, but we shared the same interests: football and music. He lived in Violet House, about a five-minute trod from where I resided.

At home, I only had a dated Dansette record player where the bass you could extract was the bare minimum. In Dwight's cottage they had a stereo with separate speakers! And a knob for the bass! Another new friend, Lloyd Massey, armed with U-Roy's *Dread in a Babylon* album, joined me one afternoon on my pilgrimage to Dwight's place to listen to our records on a modern hi-fi.

Lloyd played his album first. Always the reggae nerd, I tried to write down U-Roy's every uttering on the entire album. I failed but enjoyed myself immensely attempting to do so. Soon after, Dwight pulled the 12" version of "Waiting in the Park" by the Chantells out of its sleeve. Produced by Roy Francis at the legendary Channel One studios in Kingston, Jamaica, the rockers drum pattern compelled us to skank for all our worth. The intro from the lead singer, Samuel Bramwell, just blew me away. I had discovered a brand-new reggae talent. The toasting/rapping by Jah Berry on that track was excellent too: *Said I man sat upon ah gate in the park, said I man wait until the place get dark, man me say the girl just a skylark . . .*

We must have worn the grooves out on Dwight's vinyl record because we kept replacing the needle at the start.

Dwight's housemother finally ordered him to switch off the stereo and she kicked Lloyd and me out into the grounds. We sat on the green opposite Dwight's cottage and copied Jah Berry's toasting word for word at the top of our voices.

Then we both returned on the housemother's day off.

I expected Samuel Bramwell to emerge as reggae's next huge star. Dwight was a regular visitor to Brixton, so I handed him my hard-earned paper-round money to buy me anything that the Chantells recorded. I had "Children of Jah," "Man in Love," and "Desperate Time" in my collection. All classics.

I could hardly believe the news when I discovered in 1979 that Samuel Bramwell had been killed by Jamaican police as he committed an armed robbery at an aluminum ore factory. What a tragic loss. In Samuel's honor, I named a character after him in my young adult novel *Straight Outta Crongton*.

When Dwight left Shirley Oaks, I never saw or heard from him again. I can't help thinking the worst, but I'll be forever grateful to him for introducing me to Samuel Bramwell and the Chantells.

Years later, the opening lines to the Chantells's "Children of Jah" would still trigger me to my core: *Children of Jah cannot suffer more than what they can really bear . . .*

They brought up my early years in Holly House. For so long I had lived in denial. But I discovered along the way that my body and mind would always find a way of confronting the abuse I experienced. I suffered dreadful nightmares and was traumatized by evil characters like Bill Sikes in *Oliver*

Twist. Even the child-catcher in the children's film *Chitty Chitty Bang Bang* kept me awake at night. I imagined he had grown five meters tall, had fingers as long as a bread knife, and possessed a set of sharp teeth that clamped and crushed children's heads. His child-catcher net was full of squawking ravens.

While at Shirley Oaks, I had been physically and emotionally abused by my housemother, Miss Joyce Cook. I was struck with coal shovels, buckets, fire pokers, wooden hairbrushes, wet towels, casserole pots, bread boards, steel ladles, iron rods, curtain rails, shoe brush handles, shoe polish tins, and anything else she could lay her hands on. On one occasion, she tried to thrust a soiled bedsheet down my throat for wetting my bed. She screamed that I was the child of the devil (she attended Shirley Methodist Church and was seen as a pillar of the community). She used to threaten to confiscate my asthma inhaler if I misbehaved. She twirled it in her hands whenever I had a social worker visit.

Because of my bed-wetting and other behavioral issues, I was referred to the resident child psychiatrist. This so-called doctor ordered me to strip, and then sexually abused me as Cook waited outside. I knew even then that this wasn't normal.

I was forever in a state of terror.

Because I didn't have any family members visiting me, Miss Cook abused me with absolute impunity before I was old enough to defend myself.

Whenever social workers stopped by, I dared not say anything at all in fear of the consequences. I watched them share biscuits and sip their tea. They smoked their cigarettes and roll-ups. They discussed what TV programs they had watched. They talked about their families and what part of the country they hailed from. They shared jokes and knowing glances.

They talked about their weekend plans and asked about babies. "We're all encouraging Alex to speak more," Joyce Cook would say with a smile. "And he's such a good reader for his age. He reads the papers from front to back. We're so proud of him."

There was no place to escape to, no one to confide in. I still don't know how I survived those formative years.

When I was a young child, my only solace had been magazines.

Relatives of other children who resided with me often brought copies of *The Beano, Whizzer and Chips, The Dandy*, and my favorite, *Scorcher*. When they were thrown out or left abandoned on the dormitory floor, I would pick up these funnies and place them under my mattress.

At night, using a bicycle light, I'd chuckle beneath my bedcovers at the antics of Dennis the Menace, Minnie the Minx, the Bash Street Kids, Billy Whizz, Billy Dane, Lord Snooty, Biffo the Bear, Desperate Dan, Hot Shot Hamish, and Roy of the Rovers. It was a space where I could be the five, six, seven-year-old kid that I was. I wasn't even aware that my reading skills were accelerating remarkably because of my late-night reading.

At Christmas, I didn't have too long to wait to read *Charles Buchan's Football Monthly* or *Shoot!* magazine's soccer book (my roommates would cut out photographs of their favorite players and stick them above their beds). I still recall reading Bobby Charlton's book on the 1966 World Cup. I'd close my eyes and imagine the Wembley roar.

I reread multiple times Kenneth Wolstenholme's book about the 1970 World Cup. I'd cut out every picture of Pelé I could find. I dreamed of wearing the golden shirt of Brazil and lifting the Jules Rimet trophy.

I may have been hated in my own household, beaten up almost every day, neglected, and utterly alone, but at least the greatest footballer in the world was Black.

Even though there were very few checks on anyone who applied for work in children's care in the 1960s and '70s, I am still surprised that someone with the violent nature of Miss Cook was granted the authority to run a whole household.

The staff within my cottage, who went home to their own families following their shifts, kept silent when children as young as three were physically abused in front of their eyes.

One vivid memory is Miss Cook dragging a young white girl by her hair down the stairs. I can still hear her screams to this day.

Sunday was visiting day.

I never had a single visit from any relative during my entire stay at Shirley Oaks. I believe this caused me as much trauma and lasting damage as anything else. I was warned to be on my best behavior when relatives visited other kids in my cottage. I peered out the window, hoping that someone, anyone, would come and see me. To this day, I still struggle with intense loneliness. It can be crippling.

On one Sunday evening, when everyone had departed, I asked Miss Cook where my family was and why none of them had paid me a visit. She told me they had left me on the dock of the bay and returned to the jungle.

"You should be happy that this country gave you a home and a roof over your head. Be grateful!"

Even now, it's hard to comprehend how no one had the empathy or compassion to report the horrors of Holly House to a much higher level. I was totally unaware that these abuses were occurring in almost every other cottage in the Shirley Oaks village.

Forgive me if I do not dwell on this aspect of my life for too long, and I hope you understand why I shy away from relating more of the how-and-when details.

BOWLING LIKE MICHAEL HOLDING

....

Valentine and I loved our cricket and we both supported the West Indies team. We particularly enjoyed the humbling of England when the West Indies beat them convincingly in the UK in the 1976 series. The result was especially sweet because Tony Greig, the England captain, had promised to make the West Indies team grovel.

My cricketing heroes were Viv Richards, Clive Lloyd, Gordon Greenidge, Alvin Kallicharran, Andy Roberts, and Whispering Death, aka Michael Holding.

In school matches, I tried to imitate Michael Holding's graceful run-up to the crease and bowl. I even tried the odd bouncer. Although some deliveries strayed above head height and yards away from the wicket, on occasion I managed to bowl straight enough and claim a few wickets. I intimidated a fair few batsmen.

"Make dem jump and prance, Alex!" Valentine would will me on. "Rattle dem finger, mash up dem rib cage, and shake up their bones!"

I was branded *Demon Wheats*.

Meanwhile, Valentine, who was named after the great West Indian spinner Alf Valentine, was an elegant number-three batsman, stroking the ball to all parts of the ground.

When Valentine was dismissed, he'd march off the field cursing to himself, and throw his bat on the ground. From his bag, he'd take out a packet of custard creams, his tape recorder/player, and press play.

I'll never forget the sight of Valentine skanking to Dillinger's "Stumbling Block." I had padded up and was due to bat at number ten. It was almost impossible to focus on the game when the instrumental to "Stumbling Block" kicked in. Valentine launched into his motorbike skank, and I joined him. Backed by the Soul Syndicate Band and mixed by Prince Jammy at King Tubby's quarter tower, the music was simply irresistible.

I was dismissed for two runs on that late afternoon. Mr. Smallwood, our coach and PE teacher, wasn't impressed.

I blame it all on Dillinger and King Tubby.

In 1977, a new arts space opened in Dingwall's Road, East Croydon. It was named the Warehouse Theatre and wasn't too far from the YMCA building. It specialized in introducing works by new playwrights. At the time, I had no idea what plays were produced there or who the writers were that penned them. What I did know, from Valentine's brother-in-law Papa Cass, was that the owners of this new enterprise leased its upstairs storage space for late-night reggae jams. Naturally, Valentine and I had to be there. Even if it involved sneaking out in the middle of the night.

From Shirley Oaks, my trod along the Addiscombe Road was much longer than Valentine's—he lived only about ten minutes away. I had grown quite a bit in recent months so even if I was detected, the Shirley Oaks supervisors couldn't have stopped me. I had lost my fear of them.

Plays normally concluded around ten p.m. By eleven,

sound systems pushed the props aside to make space for a dance floor. They strung up their equipment and set up their speaker boxes. They darkened the windows with black paint. A small unlicensed bar stood at the back. If my memory serves me well, they charged a £1 entrance fee. The club was called Rainbow and you could only access it from an outside back staircase—the owners didn't want the clientele of the new club walking through the lobby and the theater.

Before Rainbow, if a reggae-head wanted to spend their late nights listening to reggae, they had to travel to Brixton. That was too far for even Valentine and me. With Rainbow, we had somewhere local where we could pay homage to the music we loved.

Papa Cass's Arrows and Jeffrey Heywood's Jah Rocker were the sound systems that played on my first night at the club. Valentine gained free admission because he helped lift Papa Cass's equipment into the space.

I had seen Jeffrey Heywood at Shirley Oaks. He dated one of the girl residents there, and he also played football with the older guys. He was a very talented baller. It was quite a thrill to have a real sound system owner among us in the Black cultural wastelands of Shirley Oaks.

One of the initial tunes Jeffrey played on my first night in Rainbow was Alton Ellis and Ranking Trevor's "You Make Me Happy." This new version of the song, produced by one of the very few female reggae producers in Jamaica, Sonia Pottinger, was exquisite. Alton Ellis's smooth vocals rode over a rockers rhythm with a deep, satisfying bass line. Valentine and I begged Jeffrey to rewind and he dutifully obliged. As I skanked away, I simply didn't care that I was outside Shirley Oaks past midnight and my curfew had long gone.

Ranking Trevor's toasting/rapping was equally captivating.

Once I bought the 12" vinyl, I can't tell you how many times I practiced Ranking Trevor's rhymes.

When I finally returned to the Shirley Oaks grounds, the complex was eerily quiet. Foxes went about their business without too much concern. I kept to the lit road as I couldn't see the mud paths through the bushes and woods. Ravens carked and flew overhead, and for some reason they gathered on the roof of the primary school. I like to think they enjoyed reggae too.

When I entered Holly House, no light was switched on except for the bulb that lit the path to the coal bunker. Miss Joyce Cook, in her long dressing gown and hair-roller cap, stood at the top of the stairs with her arms crossed. She glared at me as I climbed the steps. I paid her no mind because I knew she couldn't do anything to me anymore.

I brushed past her and went to bed. I could hear her footsteps padding along the hallway.

On the odd occasion, one of the top-ranking sound systems from South London would receive an invite to Rainbow. I remember the first time I heard Moa Anbessa from Battersea. They tested their equipment with the Tamlins's "Testify." The queue to gain entrance stretched down the stairs and along Wellesley Road. Little did I know that my future wife was a follower of Moa Anbessa. (I named my lead character after the sound system in my young adult novel *Cane Warriors*.)

Up to this day, Jeffrey, or Jeffrey Rockers as he now calls himself, still plays music for online radio and pubs in the Thornton Heath area. His love for the music hasn't waned at all. He doesn't appear to have aged either.

A SCHOOLBOY CRUSH

In the fall of 1977, Valentine's cassette player and music started gaining more attention in school. Other students wanted to listen; in particular two girls, Sandra Skyers and my crush Carol Robinson. Carol was tall and incredibly pretty. She had an elegant sway about her and was also the quickest girl in our year by a distance. She glided around the track with apparently little effort. Her PE teacher, Ms. Lane, tried to persuade her to take athletics seriously and compete more often. She was an excellent netball player too. I'm convinced Carol had the natural talent and ability to make it as an elite sportswoman. But she had other ideas. She wanted to concentrate on her schoolwork. She also wanted to listen to reggae in an empty classroom at lunchtime. My Carol character in *East of Acre Lane* was named after her. I'm glad to say she was quite chuffed.

When Valentine pressed play on his machine, I would hardly utter a word. I'm not sure if I'd even chance a glance at the two ladies present. Weak in the presence of beauty! Mind you, Valentine was always a confident brother who could chat for the both of us.

I decided to make my own mixtape. It might make it easier for me to lose my shyness if I was asked about the tracks I recorded.

First up on my mix was the 12" version of Dennis Brown's "Funny Feeling." It was the first record I'd bought by the crown prince of reggae. What a choice! The lyrics echoed my feelings toward Carol, not that she noticed: *I get that feeling inside, that funny feeling inside, gee I wanna love you . . .*

Carol simply nodded her head in time to the beat, tapped her feet, and smiled.

Trinity's toasting had me reaching for a dictionary: *And she ah gwaan like ah ginnal . . .*

What's a ginnal? I had no idea.

I consulted the dictionary. Nothing there.

Later, Valentine informed me a ginnal was a trickster or a con artist. Reggae can be educational.

I did lose my shyness a bit in those lunchtime reggae sessions. I could at least construct a sentence of five words or so. I didn't want Carol or Sandra to discover that I lived in a children's home. During any conversations about families, I'd drop my head and pray I wouldn't be asked about mine.

Many years later, Carol and I bumped into each other on the street. I revealed my schoolboy crush and she swore she'd never noticed. If only I could rewind back to that time and give a young Alex more confidence!

Valentine and I played football for our school team. I was a hard-shooting striker while Valentine was an industrious midfield player. We were a good side and we competed for all the honors available to us.

Our biggest moment came when we won the Croydon Cup final for our age group at Selhurst Park, the home of the Crystal Palace football club.

Our coach was a long-sideburned, hippie-haired, Manchester-born teacher named Mr. Keith Madeley. Often, he had to convince his colleagues that my time would be better spent playing football than in detention. I had my fair share of school fights but my usual crime for detention was displaying dissent toward teachers.

"You're an unruly, impossible boy!"

"And you're fucking ugly."

"I'll write to your parents!"

"Go ahead—I haven't got any."

On match days, I had to promise that I would serve my punishment the following afternoon. Then I wouldn't turn up or I'd simply forget. Mr. Madeley would have to put out another fire. I still owe him so much.

Our coach was committed. He always wore a loose-fitting tracksuit. Not once did I spot him in a shirt or regular trousers. He supervised all of our training, drove the minibus to away games, and was a fount of football knowledge. He was a fan of Manchester City and loved to talk about the skills of Colin Bell, Francis Lee, Mike Summerbee, Joe Corrigan, and Rodney Marsh. He was a disciple of the football coach/manager Malcolm Allison, who loved to smoke fat cigars and wear fedoras.

On those Saturday-morning trips to school grounds in and around Surrey, Valentine would pack his beloved cassette player along with his boots and shin pads.

Following one hard-fought victory, a satisfied Mr. Madeley drove us back to Shirley in the minibus. Valentine inserted a TDK cassette tape into his machine and what came out blitzed my ears: Tapper Zukie's "M.P.L.A."

The opening horn intro was a call to arms. When the bass line kicked in, I imagined marching soldiers. The lyrics were immediately printed inside my head: *Natty fling away your sorrow, natty leaving on the Black Star Line tomorrow* . . . At the time, I had no idea that M.P.L.A. was an acronym for the People's Movement for the Liberation of Angola. I couldn't even point to where Angola was on a map. I thought the Black Star Line was part of a foreign underground train network. All I knew was that I was utterly compelled to skank. And that's what I did in that small aisle within the cramped van. Mr. Madeley yelled at me to sit down.

My white teammate David Worrall remarked, "Don't know what that is but it's nothing like Status Quo."

Tapper Zukie was a huge reggae star in the mid-1970s, known for classic like "She Want a Phensic" and "Natty Dread a Weh She Want." But "M.P.L.A." will always be my fave.

TONY PARKES AND
HIS LEGENDARY AFRO

If there was one good thing about the Shirley Oaks children's home village, it was the grounds. We had orchards, playing fields, berry bushes, football pitches, stinging nettles, acorns, horse chestnuts, fir trees to climb, children's play areas, a small swimming pool, streams with connecting tunnels, a dump where we could rummage for spare bike parts, and even an area where pigs could graze.

A new friend of mine, Tony Parkes, took advantage of all this open land and ran like he was in training for the Olympics. Tony owned the best Afro in Shirley Oaks. I'm sure the barber never came within a mile of his hair. It could well have been Tony's main motivation to take up running. He very rarely stood still, and one of the few times he did, I spotted him holding close to his chest a brand-spanking-new Bob Marley and the Wailers album. The gold cover and dramatic red lettering were tempting enough. *Exodus.*

Tony may as well have been clutching the Holy Grail. Not many of us bought full albums in Shirley Oaks. I desperately wanted to listen to it. I wanted to hear it on a proper stereo system too, so I invited him up to Violet House where Dwight Grant lived.

I could barely contain my excitement as Tony pulled the vinyl out of its sleeve. The Island logo printed on the vinyl gleamed under the lights.

Tony handed the record over to Dwight, and Dwight very carefully placed it on the record deck. The tension was like the closing seconds before a heavyweight title fight. The organ kicked in. *Exodus! Movement of Jah people . . .*

It was one of those moments that I can recall vividly. I closed my eyes and just breathed in the sound. The lyrics seemed to address me directly: *Open your eyes and look within, are you satisfied with the life you're living?*

Dwight had to replace that needle at least ten times.

I soon heard the song on mainstream radio. It was everywhere—apart from the East Croydon YMCA DJ's record box.

The entire album was magical, especially "The Heathen" and "Guiltiness." I wanted to serenade every girl I fancied with "Waiting in Vain."

Many a Sunday afternoon, we'd trek up to the Addington Hills. On a clear day, the viewing platform offered a spectacular view of South London. I imagined what my life would be like if I resided in South Norwood, Norbury, Penge, Anerley, Elmers End, Crystal Palace, Sydenham, Streatham, Brixton, or Peckham. Bob Marley's "Natural Mystic" played from my cassette player. I wondered what my future could hold.

We'd encroach on the greens of the nearby golf course and steal golf balls that were close to the flag. We'd escape through the Shirley Hills and woods. We'd climb pine trees and watch pissed-off golfers searching for us. As darkness fell, we'd climb over the perimeter fence and trespass into the Pinewoods scouting complex in the hills. Here, cubs and scouts camped over the weekend and learned life-saving skills. We'd loosen the ropes and let down their tents, raid their food stores, and kick holes in their canoes. We were spotted twice but they could never catch us. I played out these scenes in my novel *Home Boys*, a narrative about kids running away from a desperate situation.

Movement of Jah people . . . Even in Shirley Oaks, I could relate to the lyrics of "Exodus."

When I hear any of the tracks today, I cannot help but think of Tony Parkes with his perfect Afro running around Shirley Oaks.

GOLD CUP DANCE

....

In early 1978, Valentine and I regularly attended the Sir Philip Game Centre youth club in Addiscombe, Croydon. There, we played table football, pool, badminton, and table tennis. They also had a boxing gym on-site. Once, I spied through the window and watched a young Frank Bruno mutilating a heavy bag.

Reggae-heads practiced their skanking in a small room where the resident boom-box guy would entertain us with his selection of music. I cannot recall his name, but I'll always remember this boom-box DJ pressing pause on his huge machine and introducing the next tune: "And this track is by the sweet-granulated Lincoln Sugar Minott! Voiced at Channel One studios and mixed at King Tubby's quarter tower!"

I knew what a sound system control tower looked like, but King Tubby's quarter tower? I could only imagine the great man's mixing desk.

Near the lobby, we picked up flyers advertising karate classes, netball matches, lost cats, jumble sales, five-a-side football matches, music lessons, and so much more. It was rare to collect a flyer in this corner of Croydon that promoted a top-ranking sound system clash in South London.

The venue was Nettleford Hall in West Norwood. The

sound systems competing were from Brixton the Rum Drinker, Sir Coxsone, from southeast London the heavyweight dub champion Jah Shaka, and the people's choice from Battersea, Moa Anbessa. They would be competing for a gold cup.

A real gold cup? I wondered. I had a pleasure overload.

Not many reggae-heads I knew had ever heard Jah Shaka play, but the fables and myths about the earth-rumbling bass filled me to the brim with anticipation.

"Shaka's bass is so deep it'll wake up your granny's granny," a reggae-head insisted. "His speaker boxes are tall like a Brixton tower block!"

"Did you see that film with King Kong brawling with Godzilla? That's how Shaka bass feels like."

When we boarded the 68 bus from East Croydon, the top deck was already filled with reggae fans. It was rowdy. Two boom boxes were in competition with each other. We climbed up to Crystal Palace and Beulah Hill before descending Knights Hill. I can't remember paying bus fare on that journey; the conductor looked relieved when we departed. (I included a similar scene in my novel *Brixton Rock*.)

We headed for Nettleford Hall. There was an almighty scrum outside and there were reggae-heads as far as I could see. I had never seen so much red, gold, and green. The doorman had trouble collecting the entrance fee. Ravers surged this way and that. People's toes got stepped on. Curses cut the air. The doorframe and the windows shook as one sound system tested their set. I spotted two girls who had fainted being carried outside. They were propped up against a graveyard's railings.

"Wake up, sister!"

Valentine and I finally made it inside. I'm not sure if my feet touched the ground as we did so. We looked up to the ceiling. There was a spaghetti junction above us, a mass of cables and wires connected to the sound system control towers. Stacks of speaker boxes filled the walls. Valentine pointed out where Jah Shaka had set up and we barged in that direction.

Jah Shaka himself, shorter than I'd expected, carefully and patiently connected jack plugs to the amplifiers. The aluminum casing glinted blue from the live valves. The transistor was big enough to make it part of the furniture. It was something out of science fiction. He used brown masking tape to add extra safety for the speaker cable connections. There must have been around one hundred pairs of eyes watching Jah Shaka's preparations.

Finally, his turntable spun. He wiped the needle with his index finger and a sonic boom–like sound reverberated around the hall. There was a long hush as Jah Shaka selected the first 12" track to test his system.

The needle dropped. I opened my mouth. My heart beat faster. The midrange and tweeter boxes kicked in first. Percussion and drums. The vocal came in: *Every man do his thing a little way different. Don't matter what color race or creed that he may be . . .*

The bass dropped. Or something not of this world fell to earth and made its way to Nettleford Hall. Over forty years later, I still have much difficulty describing that moment. It was like a fat dinosaur suffering a severe asthma attack very close to your eardrum. It was utterly overwhelming. An assault on the senses. A defibrillator moment that was unforgettable. There were expressions of astonishment all around me. Valentine and I shared a long look. Neither of us could find the words. I wanted to break out in a mad skank but there was no room to do so.

The track was produced by the masterful Dennis Bovell,

with Janet Kay on backing vocals. I'd very much like to know who played bass on that production.

I can't recall who was victorious in that sound clash. I do remember drink cans and bottles of Lucozade dropping off Shaka's speaker boxes. Following the event, I also recall the driver refusing to move as so many reggae-heads had squeezed onto his 68 bus. We had to trod home.

CHURCH VS. FOOTBALL

....

For some reason, when I was eight years old it was decided by my housemother that I was a Catholic. To this day, I have no idea how they arrived at that conclusion because as far as I know, neither of my parents ever practiced the Catholic faith. I have read all my social services files and never found any references to Catholicism.

I guessed something sinister was afoot. This strange man with a wide grin visited me at my cottage and presented me with a Bible, a prayer book, and blue rosary beads. He said he couldn't wait to welcome me at his church, Our Lady of the Annunciation. It was about a twenty-minute walk from where I lived near Ashburton Park. The whole idea freaked the fuck out of me, but at least I'd be able to *see* life outside the Shirley Oaks complex, I figured.

I wanted to play in the soccer games that took place on the Shirley Oaks grounds every Sunday morning. Someone always had a hard leather football, especially after Christmas. Bushes were our touchlines and pullovers and anoraks served as goalposts. The lunchtime call from housemothers was our final whistle, and the referee was usually the player no one wanted to mess with. Fouls were never given if the aggressor was bigger than you. If you nutmegged anybody your reward was a slap on the back of the head.

Reluctantly, off to church I went. At least I received a pair of new shoes, a white shirt, and a pair of blue slacks.

In one sermon, the priest assured the congregation that everyone was welcome in God's house. He explained that the church and where he lived were all God's residence. *Let the children come unto me,* the Lord said.

This sounds promising, I thought.

When I had the chance to speak to the priest, I asked him if it was possible for me to live in God's house. I promised I wouldn't take up too much space. I just needed a shelf for my comics and a football, if I was ever given one. The priest said it didn't quite work like that. I thought, *Fuck you! And what's with the black dress thing?*

I never attended the church again, but I did post something smelly, something canine, through the priest's letter box.

Instead of listening to priest's sermons, I'd play truant every Sunday morning and spend my 2p collection money on a gobstopper or a juicy-fruit sweet. If I had 4p I'd buy myself a jamboree bag that had sherbet inside. I'd wander into Ashburton Park and watch guys playing football. Sometimes they invited me to play. I had to be careful not to scuff my polished shoes. When I arrived home, I'd take off my beads and place them in a shoe for next Sunday.

My housemother discovered my skiving one day and beat the devil out of me from one end of the dormitory to the other. Then she dragged me to the hallway and repeated the dose. But I didn't care—if I couldn't live in God's house, then I wasn't attending any of the priest's services. *Fuck them.* They were boring anyway. I also thought they were a bit mean with the bread rations they offered to the congregation. Why couldn't they serve toast?

In the end, they gave up trying to convince me that the

church would save my sinful Black soul. I figured that hell couldn't be much worse than the life I was living anyway.

In the fall of 1977, I bumped into the weird man with the ready smile outside Fred Dawes's newsagents on Wickham Road. "Why have you given up on the Lord?" he asked me.

He wasn't expecting my answer: "Him ah knot-up him head, him ah spread him bed, him ah Jesus Dread!"

The man looked at me as if I were possessed by Beelzebub himself. He hurried on his way, crossing himself and shaking his head.

I had just quoted Trinity from his huge reggae hit "Jesus Dread." Produced by Yabby You and mixed at King Tubby's quarter tower, it was one of those tunes where you just had to wiggle a toe or shake a leg. The bass line played its own melody, and my God, when I heard and felt that bass blow out of Papa Cass's bass speaker box, I was in heaven.

EXPELLED

······································

Whatever school I attended, teachers were forever instructing me to ignore racist insults, taunts, and bigoted aggression. At one secondary school, someone wrote *Alex the Wog* on the blackboard. When the teacher arrived, she simply rubbed it off and said, "Don't let it get to you, Alex, they're just being childish."

"Would it get to you if I called you a whore?" I countered.

I had suffered blatant racism from as early as I could remember.

Playing football for my school team when I was fourteen, I missed a good scoring opportunity one afternoon. The defender covering me remarked, "Wog-a-matter, feeling all browned off this morning? Didn't you have your coon flakes this morning? Don't worry, you might feel all white tomorrow."

I threw a right cross and a left hook and he dropped to the ground. I was about to deliver a boot to his back when the referee and the opposing teammates intervened. I was sent off, but they had to drag me from the field. My tormentor promised vengeance as he was helped back to the changing rooms.

I said, "Anytime."

Here I am at one of the various secondary schools I attended

Teachers made sure we didn't clash after the game.

We met after school a week or so later in the Addington Hills. He had brought a crew with him, all leather jackets, buckled boots, greased-up hair, white T-shirts, and knuckle-dusters. None of them looked remotely like Elvis Presley. Valentine and a few other school friends backed me up. I wanted to fight him man to man, but an almighty fist-to-fist melee kicked off. Before we knew it, sirens were blaring.

Kids scattered in all directions.

I was quickly arrested (I think the police strategy was to

arrest all the Black people) but Valentine managed to escape to the woods. For more than two hours I refused to answer any questions from the police.

"What's your address?" they barked. "Where do you live? Who are your parents?"

I finally gave up my silence: "I ain't got no fucking parents."

They all looked at each other.

"Are you from the home?" one of them asked.

I nodded.

Joyce Cook had to come and claim me.

Once I recognized her embarrassment and awkwardness, I cheered up.

Because I had been in a school uniform and was seen by the authorities as the chief initiator of the whole affair, I was immediately expelled. The white guy who had racially abused me received a warning about his future conduct.

I served my expulsion by playing all the reggae records I owned plus the ones that Valentine had accumulated. In the afternoons I'd ride my bike (which I had assembled from spare parts I found at the dump) around the Shirley Oaks grounds.

When I felt more adventurous, I'd pedal to Elmers End, Beckenham, Penge, Anerley, and Crystal Palace. Then I'd bomb down Anerley Hill praying that the brakes I'd salvaged would work.

A Shirley Oaks brother named David Miller kindly offered his 12" vinyl tracks for me to listen to; he was also a committed reggae-head. The first one I played was "Loving Pauper/Judgement Time" by Ruddy Thomas and Trinity.

I could relate to the lyrics where a poor young man wonders how he will treat the lady of his desires on a date.

Trinity's toasting was phenomenal. I wrote down his rap and practiced it every day, trying to pronounce every word correctly: *Went to the market to buy ah liccle food, the price of the food mek me gwaan like me rude cah this ah judgement time, ahey . . .*

There was no accommodation for my missed education while I served my expulsion. The staff was happy for me to play my music in an empty dormitory or dining room. Valentine stopped by now and again, and he helped me build a wooden record box. I called it Alex's Treasure Chest.

I'd return to the school grounds to watch Valentine play football or cricket. (I'm convinced that if it wasn't for his addiction to reggae music, Valentine could have played cricket professionally.) PE teachers warned me off, but I stood my ground. "What are you gonna do?"

School was always a challenge for me, though I preferred to attend rather than be at home alone. Loneliness was my ever-present and greatest enemy. Reggae helped combat that.

No school in the Croydon borough accepted me for four months. As I was considered a Catholic, they even attempted to have me enrolled in St. Joseph's College in West Norwood. It would have meant two long bus rides—from Shirley to East Croydon, and then I'd have to take a number 68 to the school.

It didn't take the school long to utterly reject the idea. I would never have gone there anyway—they played rugby.

Finally, following a desperate plea from my social worker, Monks Hill Comprehensive School in Addington agreed to take me in. Addington was a good trod south of the Addington Hills. I had to jump on a 130 bus. It seemed colder there than any other place in Surrey. Shirley Oaks kids christened it the "wilderness."

The uniform was horrible: a green pullover, tie, and blazer. Not the kind of thing for a cool reggae-head. I wanted to get expelled again just so I wouldn't have to wear it.

When I joined my classes, the teachers didn't even bother trying to educate me. There weren't any expectations of me. I often had a desk in a corner, took no part in any classroom discussion, and spent my time writing down lyrics from the reggae toasters I loved. I studied U-Roy, I-Roy, Dennis Alcapone, and many others. In technical drawing class, instead of learning geometry and working out angles, I spent my time designing reggae album sleeves.

If I could've sat down for a reggae A-level, I'm confident I would've passed it and gone on to Reggae University.

My English was better than most. I could read anything anyone put in front of me, but it was never encouraged. I remember reading J.B. Priestley's *An Inspector Calls* and becoming totally engrossed in the narrative. The young girl who dies in the story was a sufferah. I related to her. When I raised my hand to ask a question about a particular aspect of the work, the English teacher almost collapsed in shock. "Alex! Alex! I'm so glad that you're engaging with the text. What does the story tell you about the attitude of the rich toward the poor?"

"That they hate us!"

"I wouldn't say *hate*," she replied. "Perhaps indifferent to her suffering."

"Nope," I argued, "they hate us. Why do you think that is?"

She told me it was a play, and I wondered if it was ever staged at the Warehouse Theatre in East Croydon. I would have gone and watched it.

At lunchtime in Monks Hill, I entertained myself in an empty classroom listening to my own cassette player. Other kids kept their distance. My reputation came before me. The school authorities seemed to be happy that I simply turned up for registration.

However, there was one stunning reason why I kept attending Monks Hill Comprehensive School and didn't play truant. Her name was Janice Powell. Tall and elegant, she had an Afro that a master sculptor could not have bettered. Tony Parkes had a rival.

I agonized for days and weeks over how to introduce myself to her, but I simply couldn't beat away my shyness. I couldn't come up with anything to say to her, so I decided to buy her a 12" record—someone had informed me she liked listening to lovers' rock.

I guessed I couldn't go wrong with 15 16 17's "Suddenly Happiness." It was the first time in my life I had bought two copies of the same record. My paper-round money was coming to good use.

15 16 17 were a very popular vocal trio in the late 1970s. Almost every young Black female who loved reggae wanted to form a singing group and emulate 15 16 17, Brown Sugar, Black Harmony, or Sister Love. "Suddenly Happiness" itself is a classic of the genre, the smooth lead vocal and harmonies gliding over a gentle lovers' rock beat.

When I presented Janice with her gift, she smiled warmly and thanked me. I even managed a few words. Unfortunately, I didn't stay long enough at Monks Hill to establish any kind of friendship with her. I was expelled once again for fighting.

My guardians didn't know what to do with me. The Borstal youth detention center or some other secure unit was threatened. I made up my mind that if this was their solution, I'd simply run away. (This was the seed for my novel *Home Boys*.)

STRICTLY COME SKANKING

On a Thursday evening at the Sir Philip Game Centre in Addiscombe, no player scored a goal on the football table. No sound of ping-pong balls echoed from the table-tennis hall. You couldn't hear the swipe and thwack of a badminton racket. The heavy slap of dominoes was absent, and nobody lined up a shot on the pool table. No noses pressed against the meshed glass window to watch the boxing training.

Everyone was crammed into a side room at the club to take part or watch the latest skanking contest. Whoever owned the best boom box was the DJ (the criteria was quite simple—who had the heaviest bass line? This serious dispute was always resolved at the last minute).

In this small, sweaty room with minimum ventilation, perspiration dripping from our brows, Valentine and I perfected our revving motorbike, pleading to Jah, and stepping basketball moves. Other skankers rolled up their jeans and pulled on their red, gold, and green wristbands.

The eternal winner of this skanking contest was my bredren from Shirley Oaks, David Miller. He seemed to defy gravity as he skanked away on one foot. You thought he'd topple over—but no! There he was in perfect control of his body as the crowd hollered his name. I soooo much wanted to push him over!

He triumphed one evening skanking to Pat Kelly and Trinity's "I'm So in Love with You/Jammin' So." Pat Kelly's controlled falsetto grooved over a reggae dancehall beat. Trinity was full of memorable catch phrases on this track: *Why you're jamming so, sister* and *Rain ah fall, breeze ah blow, no one should be out ah door . . .*

Valentine and I tried to match David as he skanked closer and closer to the floor. It involved bopping your backside in the air, rocking your knees in time to the beat, and tapping the ground with your index fingers in a drumming motion (don't try this at home). You had to be nimble, supple, and possess the balance of a prima ballerina.

The boom-box DJ pressed pause and asked the crowd who they wanted to cheer for. Needless to say, David was declared the winner once again and I skulked home complaining of a pulled muscle.

In the late 1970s, every young male reggae-head I knew wanted to dress like Gregory Isaacs. You were considered the definition of cool if you sported a Gabicci or a Cecil Gee top complete with a suede collar and trimmings. If you boasted a black felt bowler hat, slim slacks, a red, gold, and green belt, and crocodile-skin shoes, then you were almost on the same level as the "Cool Ruler" himself.

The only thing was, no one could sing quite like Gregory Isaacs. His delicate vocals were distinctive and effortless. Gregory's appearance in the *Rockers* film cemented him as a reggae icon (he even had a cool walk that I tried to imitate), not just for his singing and songwriting, but for his fashion sense too. I cannot remember any other reggae artist having the same impact as he did on style.

There were untold Gregory impersonators who attended

the Bali Hai club on a Sunday night. It was situated on the London Road in Streatham opposite the Common in the same building complex as the ice rink. To reach the venue, I had to take a bus to East Croydon and then jump on a 109 or 130 to Streatham.

There was a dress code at the door, so "cruffs" or "ragamuffins" wearing jeans, military clothing, tracksuit tops, trainers, and the like were refused admission.

"You cyan't come in dressed like yuh waan start ah war!" said the doorman to a sufferah clothed in fatigues.

Soferno B, a Brixton sound system, was the resident sound. Their DJ was a heavy-set bearded brother nicknamed Big Yout'. Others called him Chabba Yout'. Every young reggae-head admired him because Big Yout' cruised around South London in a top-of-the-range 3.5 Rover. He boasted thick rope gold chains around his neck, and more bling sexed up his broad fingers. For reggae-heads like me, the Chabba Yout's of this world were like A-list movie stars.

The club itself was decorated in fake palm trees and bamboo furnishings. It was a ram-jam affair every Sunday evening. Girls wore their perfume and brothers slapped on too much aftershave.

On my first night at Bali Hai, I wasn't dressed like Gregory Isaacs, but I did wear a zip-up cardigan with no suede trimmings whatsoever, dark slacks, and a pair of black moccasins. Luckily for me, it was dark enough inside for me to be considered half cool.

Of course, Big Yout' played a number of Gregory Isaacs tunes. The one I loved most was "Mr. Brown." The song tells the story of a young romantic hero informing the father of his girl that he's dating her before getting married. It's classic Gregory and it launched me into a frenzy of buying anything the singer released.

I couldn't dress like Gregory, yet at least I had his music.

I often missed my last bus back home to Shirley Oaks, but I didn't care. I could now say, *I raved at Bali Hai!* They'd have to dig up my grave and carry my coffin if I was ever to be seen again at a YMCA disco.

PRESSURE DROPPING

....

Following my third expulsion, no school in the London borough of Croydon would accept me. I had just celebrated my sixteenth birthday when it was decided by social workers and senior staff at Shirley Oaks to send me back to Brixton, where I first lived with my father as a baby, to reside in a hostel. "You'll like it there," said a housefather. "More of your kind are there. As you love fighting so much, you can go and fight them."

I was going to tell him to fuck himself with his Jethro Tull and Cat Stevens albums, but I didn't want to spend a further second in his company.

Apart from my comic collection that included *The Beano* and *Scorcher*, my cassette player, and of course my precious reggae records, I didn't have too much to pack for my journey to Elm Park, just off Brixton Hill.

I'll never forget the bumpy ride in my social worker's Morris Minor. For my Croydon friends to visit me they'd have to jump on a 109 bus that took forever to get through the traffic on the London Road.

At this point I still hadn't read my social services files. The thought occurred to me that I might walk past my parents in Brixton without realizing it.

I was taken to my ground-floor room at number 15, Elm Park. It was a small town house with two upper floors and I was given a brief tour. In the kitchen, there was half a bottle of milk in the fridge, five slices of bread, a lump of cheese, a Weetabix box, and a packet of flour in the cupboard. Cats often fought at night in the overgrown garden. Tarzan would have gotten lost in there.

I remember a huge poster of Dennis Brown that hung in the communal room on the first floor. It advertised his appearance at the Rainbow, Finsbury Park. I loved that.

My single bed had missing feet on one side and was propped up by paint tins. The walls were scarred and bruised. The carpet was as thin as a page and I had no dressing table or wardrobe. My social worker presented me with a tiny black-and-white television set that only broadcast BBC1. I placed it on a cardboard box and sighed because Sunday cricket was usually broadcast on BBC2. They often featured Viv Richards and Ian Botham's county team, Somerset. *Damn!*

Later, I'd decorate the walls with flyers of reggae raves, club nights, and dances.

I was never taught any life skills like cooking, budgeting, or preparing for job interviews. No one offered me career advice, though I was given directions to the unemployment exchange. I was granted a meager weekly allowance (which I spent mostly on reggae records) until I found work.

As I sat on the bed that first day, loneliness attacked me.

Where's my mother, father, family? Why was I even born? Why is my life so fucking hard? Where is the mercy of this so-called fucking God? He's having a laugh at my expense. One day, I'm gonna smash your stained-glass windows and burn down one of your churches. Then you might know I exist.

I held back my tears until my social worker departed.

That was his one and only visit—if I wanted any support, I had to make my way down to the area three office on Herne Hill Road and ask for the duty social worker.

I took out my cassette player and pressed play. Sugar Minott's "Hard Time Pressure" echoed my lived experience. The lyrics cut through to my core: *Some can't take it, but they can't leave it . . .*

At Elm Park, I was reintroduced to Joyce Smith and Carol Brown, who I had befriended at Shirley Oaks. My spirits revived a notch. Joyce welcomed me to my new home with fried dumplings and sugared milk.

Sharing the dumplings with me was a tall, skinny brother I didn't know. He wasn't a resident of Elm Park; he seemed to be a friend of everybody and lived up near the New Park Road council estate. His name was Errol Findlay.

"What far-out cold bumpkin land you come from?" he teased as soon as I opened my mouth. "You sound whiter than the people who read the news, to raatid!"

"I'm from Surrey," I replied. "Shirley Oaks. Same place as Joyce and Carol."

"They sound . . . at least ah liccle Black," Errol laughed. "You speak like you wax Prince Charles's Daimler! You better lose that tone of voice around these sides."

When we had finished our meal, Errol took it upon himself to be my Brixton tour guide. He advised me where to get my hair cut (Raymond's Barbershop on Stonhouse Street near Clapham Common), where to buy trendy clothes, and where to score weed. He also warned me about "Babylon," the police. He said I would have to change my "country-bumpkin walk" and learn to trod like a Black man. He showed me Tumper's store on Railton Road where I could buy my West Indian snacks.

Errol gave me a briefing on the top sound systems in Brixton: Soferno B, the Brixton King Tubby (who often tested his equipment in the forecourt of Cowley Estate on Brixton Road), Neville King, V Rocket, and the top-ranking party/blues sound, Studio One.

Feeling slightly better about my situation once I returned to my new home, I rewound my cassette tape and replayed Sugar Minott's "Hard Time Pressure": *Some are forced to stay under it . . .*

I knew that life would never be the same.

A HUNGRY MAN
IS AN ANGRY MAN

....

Reality licked me hard in my first weeks living in Brixton. I failed abysmally at trying to budget whatever money I had. Most of it was spent in Soferno B's record shack at the junction of Atlantic Road and Coldharbour Lane (those guys never offered credit or a discount!). Often, I went three or four days where I hadn't a single penny to my name. I had zero food in the larder and nothing in the fridge. I did make the trek to the area three office on Herne Hill Road, and on a couple of occasions the duty social worker offered me a handout of five pounds or so. "Go and do some shopping," he urged.

I might have bought a loaf of bread and a small box of cereal. Nothing more than that. Sometimes there was enough cash left over to buy a beef patty and chips at the fish-and-chip shop down Brixton Hill. But I was addicted to buying reggae records. Also, to add another complication, on Friday nights I'd head down to the Brixton Frontline on Railton Road with Errol and score a small draw of weed. Once, I went down there on my own and purchased a draw of thyme and mixed herbs. I smoked it (with half a cigarette) anyway.

"Wheats," Errol said, "what's wrong wid you? Don't you

know the bloodclaat difference between collie weed and thyme? You're coming like a raasclaat Worzel Gummidge, to raatid!"

If you had to step down into a derelict basement to purchase your "collie," you passed idlers, badmen, madmen, and the permanently stoned. One evening, I had an argument with a guy who claimed the world was about to end.

"When the two sevens clash," he ranted, "it will be the end! The very end! Repentance is a must!" His views were not too different from the priest I'd encountered as a child. "Jesus died because of you!" he went on. "So repent!"

The Frontline was always lively. Reggae music was constant. The banter, cussing, and mickey-taking was relentless.

"Where are your shoes?" a badman asked a barefoot sufferah. "This is England! In Ingland man wear shoes. Man don't walk street with their bunions outta door! Go find some shoes!"

"But wait!" another would say. "When the last time soap kissed your skin? Eh? Eh?"

Toasters practiced their rhymes and the sufferahs nodded and voiced their approval.

If ah sufferah want to make ah dime
Him forward to de Frontline
But you must sell de ital weed
And not the mixed herbs and thyme
Otherwise, you're looking for ah jook anytime . . .

The hustlers wrapped up the goods in betting shop paper, and Errol forever advised me to smell what I had just bought.

"That's not a two-pound draw! No, man! Give me ah liccle more!"

"You have plenty, mon. Best collie weed inna Brixton!"

"Best collie weed inna Brixton? It's not even the best collie weed in this damn dutty basement!"

"You're making me poor, bredren. Nuff bush me ah give you!"

"Nuff bush? I've seen more bush in a baby's armpit!"

I wasn't in Kansas anymore.

On my hungry days, I'd listen out in the early morning for the chink of the milk float. When it passed my hostel, I'd chase after it and plunder two or three pints. On lucky days, I'd manage to pilfer a loaf of bread. The milkman never caught me or even spotted me. Dry bread and sugared milk filled my belly for the best part of a week.

When I didn't catch the milk float or if I overslept, I'd walk down to the Woolworths store on Brixton High Street and shoplift a couple packets of custard creams or chocolate bourbons. Angel cake was a favorite too. I was once seen pocketing my booty under my jacket, but they could never catch me.

The convenience store on Elm Park was another option. One early evening, I managed to steal a packet of flour that Joyce gleefully used to make fried dumplings. A Croydon friend of mine, who shall remain nameless, rushed into said shop and came out with a large bottle of whiskey with the owner in hot pursuit. Anyone who emerged from number 15, Elm Park, was banned from the store. We had a long trod to buy our cigarette papers.

Errol and his bredren loved strong Special Brew and Tennent's beers. I was never a lager drinker. Soft fizzy drinks or Lucozade were my thing. But getting food supplies was a constant stress.

When we had friends around, weed would be smoked,

brothers got "charged," jokes were laughed at, the bass knobs on the boom boxes were set to the max, and then everybody would suffer the munchies.

We'd play cards not for money, but for dares. Black Jack was the game of choice. Sometimes we played with two packs. If you got hit with four black jacks, you were obliged to pick up twenty cards. If you lost a hand and refused to perform the dare, you'd have to suffer a beatdown.

On one occasion, I had to go out in the street in the middle of a sunny afternoon and "crub" down a lamppost like it was a hot girl. *Dirty Dancing* had nothing on me. A passing Black woman muttered something under her breath about the unwashed and ungodly.

Another bredren was forced to wear one of Joyce's frocks, place a saucepan on his head, and step down to the corner shop to buy cigarette papers. I had to take out my asthma inhaler because I laughed so hard.

I'd wake up with a head full of fog. The loaf of bread that I stole two days ago would be no more.

Feeling peckish one morning, I reached for the bag of flour. There is nothing worse in this world than a seriously stoned brother trying to roll and fry dumplings. Joyce was not happy.

Sugar Minott was a constant presence on my cassette player. "Man Hungry" perfectly reflected my very peckish experiences at sixteen. The lyrics were powerful too: *Because of the rich-men administration, it has polluted many nation . . .* If Sugar recorded this today, the words would not be dated.

Some might question my choices, but I'd argue that tracks like "Man Hungry" were my brain food. They helped to shape and guide the future writer in me.

BRIXTON BLUES NIGHT

· ·

Two months or so after I had settled into Elm Park, we decided to host a party. The King Solomon sound system, owned by a dread named Trevor and operated by Shirley Oaks old-boy Barry Burnett, agreed to play the music.

We cleared the first-floor communal room, and Trevor's speaker boxes and amplifiers moved in. Barry flicked through his record collection, deciding what and when to play that night.

Money was pooled and someone drove to the local cash-and-carry to purchase crates of cheap beer and other popular drinks of the day, including Snowball, Pink Lady, Thunderbird, and Cherry B. They would be sold at inflated prices at the makeshift bar in the kitchen. We put the word out and expected a ram-jam crowd.

I invited Valentine down from Croydon. He was excited—his first Brixton blues party. We decided that we'd dress up in black felt Stetsons, Farah slacks, and imitation silk flower shirts (if only we had camera phones back in the late '70s!). We almost looked like twins, but we were prepped and ready to meet the ladies arriving for the dance.

Trevor and Barry completed their final checks on the sound system and began to spin music from around ten p.m., the bass lines vibrating the walls. A steady flow of partygoers and reggae-heads started arriving around eleven p.m. The vibe was nice, spliffs were inhaled, and drinks flowed. Valentine and I tried to make eye contact with the pretty girls in the rave. Sweet boys styled gold teeth, thick gold rope chains, and reptile-skin shoes. Seasoned herbalists wrapped five-paper joints in the dark (how did they manage that?).

My single bed was covered in jackets and coats. The temperature rose and windows were opened.

Louisa Mark's "6, Six Street" trilled out from the speakers around one a.m. It was the mega lovers' rock hit of its day. The horns intro and Louisa's opening—*Iffff, if only you told me yourself*—just completely hooked us. Every male in the dance looked for a partner to crub with. The 12" version of the song went on for seven minutes or so. If you were lucky, you could swap phone numbers, arrange a date, whisper sweet things in your dance partner's ear, and drain a Cherry B together. Hands caressed shoulders and slid down backs. Torsos were pressed together. Couples smooched as one entity, dipping the hip and tracing the figure eight.

Sheer bliss.

Then: a fierce banging on the front door.

Valentine and I looked out an upstairs window. There were two police vans parked outside our hostel. Three police officers stood by our front door.

"Don't let the beast in!" someone hollered. "Go 'way, dutty Babylon!"

The police ordered us to turn down the music. Everyone wondered why they had arrived in such force. Neighbors appeared in dressing gowns outside their homes.

Valentine and I rushed downstairs to defend the front door. I fretted about the police breaking through my bedroom window.

"Resist the dutty Babylon!" another cried.

Trevor switched the sound system off and went outside to try to reason with the police. An officer said they had intelligence that cannabis was being smoked on the premises and alcohol was being sold. They must be allowed entry to investigate.

A group of us braced ourselves by the front door. Ravers jostled for position to peer through the windows.

"Oink off, you dutty fucking pig!"

Another van arrived. *SPG* was marked on its roof—Special Patrol Group. Some of the officers were in plainclothes. They brought with them some sort of metal battering ram and rushed the front door. I'll never forget the sound of the door panels breaking and the latch lock dropping to the floor. The police stormed the hostel.

Valentine and I found ourselves on the street fighting officers and trying to resist arrest. I spotted Joyce clubbing a plainclothes policeman with the heel of her shoe. Screams, curses, and chaos surrounded us. Windows were smashed. Truncheons beat my head and battered my back. I threw right crosses and left hooks. I think I connected twice. I lashed out with my feet.

"You fucking swine head!"

"Get your trotters off me!"

"Leave me alone and go fuck your pagan self!"

Before I knew it, I was flung into the back of a "beast wagon" and handcuffed. Valentine was thrown in with me. A Rastaman was launched on top of us. He screamed as a few of his locks were pulled from his scalp. Blood dripped on my imitation silk flower shirt. Boots were pressed on our heads to keep us still. The dread squinted in acute pain as I sniffed the dusty floor.

We were driven down to the Brixton police station. I felt every bump and vibration on the road through my cheeks and forehead. I cannot even remember if I was formally charged. What I do recall is that I was taken downstairs and thrown in a cell. They slammed the door shut.

All was quiet for the next two hours or so. Sometime after four a.m., I heard footsteps. Many footsteps. I heard keys opening the cell door next to me.

"Go fuck yourself! Babylon will fall! You dutty bloodclaat!"

It was Trevor's voice. I pressed my ear to the wall. What I heard next will probably stay with me to the end of my days: The sound of Trevor being viciously beaten. His wails. His defiance. His cries. His courage. His pain. Every now and again, they'd slam his body against a wall. I felt the tremors.

There was nothing I could do but listen.

If that was my fate, I wanted it over and done with. The waiting was unbearable. For me, it was the most traumatic moment of the night.

Half an hour later, they came for me. I decided to put up no resistance. I curled myself into a ball, covered my face with one hand, and protected my genitals with the other. They punched and hacked at me for a few minutes, laughing all the while.

"They're not so fucking tough when they're on their own, are they?"

"There are too many of 'em," another cop said. "My dear mum doesn't feel safe walking the streets. Black muggers living all around her."

"We'll make it safer for her."

"Fucking coons and their jungle music."

"Why can't they be like normal people and play records on a stereo?"

"Thatcher should put them all on a banana boat and send them back to where the fuck they come from."

I detested my housemother for beating me as a defenseless child in Holly House, but this was on another level. A primal rage filled me. That night I wanted to kill a policeman. I would have accepted any sentence passed down to me. *If only I could confront one of them on their own.*

Years later, that emotion would drive the actions of my character Coffin Head in my novel *East of Acre Lane.* It may be fiction, but is based on a lived reality. I wrote his scenes interacting with the police with brimstone and fire in my belly.

Coffin Head kicked the bedroom door closed, kissed his teeth, and covered his face with the palms of his hands. "Beast arrested me, innit. I dunno where de raas dey tek me. All I know so is dey did boot me up inna cell an' dey didn't even charge me, to raatid. After dat, dey fling me in de beast wagon, tek me to Wandswort' Road, an' fling me 'pon de kerb like how dem council sweeper fling rubbish bag."

He who feels it knows it.

Once they discovered that I was still a juvenile, I was released around eleven a.m. the next morning. I wearily trod up Brixton Hill. Trevor's wailing continued to ring inside my head.

When I reached home, I found that my bedroom window had been smashed and the lock on my door was busted. Later that day, Valentine helped me with my repairs.

"So, this is living in Brixton, Wheats," he said. "I cry for you. Can't you find a decent place in Croydon?"

"Lambeth social services don't run any hostels in Croydon," I responded. "Where could I live?"

"You could coch with me for a while."

I considered Valentine's offer. The truth was, I loved the tension, the music, the jeopardy, and the drama of Brixton.

LIVING ON THE FRONTLINE

In my early days in Brixton, I would often follow my new bredren Errol to the Frontline on Railton Road. He would buy his two-pound draw of weed, build a long spliff with five Rizla papers (there were no long cigarette papers available in those days), and offer me a puff. Sometimes this would almost make me bring up my one-slice-of-bread breakfast.

I had entered another world.

Many of the houses on this stretch of Railton Road were in a state of decay; some were squats. In other dwellings, I couldn't work out who lived here or there because people arrived and departed like it was a train terminal.

Windows were covered with corrugated fencing. Damp patches were visible on the brickwork. Overhead wires provided electricity from adjacent properties. Weed smokers, sufferahs, idlers, the unemployed, lost hippies, crazies, ranters, sound system "toasters," and the curious mingled with the occasional crime lord. Reggae music boomed out from upstairs windows. The unshoed and the raggedy-clothed danced in the streets. The odd gay couple strolled by. Every second person seemed to puff from a "big head." Someone always went by chanting lines from the Bible.

"Repent! Repent!"

A top-ranking weed hustler wore gold sovereigns on his fingers. A thick rope gold chain decorated his neck. A beaver-skin hat sat on his head. A Cecil Gee or Gabicci top wrapped his trunk. If it was cold, he'd wear a long camel-skin or cashmere coat. He walked with a bounce, swagger, and a dip. Confidence flowed from him. He'd side-eye you while flicking out his ratchet knife.

A cannabis connoisseur was spoiled for choice.

I soon became familiar with the different terms for weed: *collie, sinsemilla, lambs bread, bush, marijuana, herb* . . . I could go on.

Sometimes I spotted suited white men emerging from expensive cars with tinted windows, purchasing their weed, and driving away at high speed. In the evening, ladies of the night appeared on the scene, carefully monitored by their pimps in parked cars.

Every weekend there were reggae raves, blues dances, and parties all over South London and beyond. I'm convinced Brixton's Frontline supplied the vast majority of weed for those all-night sessions. Smoking a spliff at a dance was as common as sipping a can of Coca-Cola.

Errol tried to school me in wrapping a five-paper spliff in a dimly lit dance, but I never achieved it.

The Frontline fascinated me, so even when I wasn't purchasing herb, I'd walk down there to observe. There was always good reggae to listen to.

Gradually, I got to know a few of the faces.

One crime lord spotted me, bought me a patty from Tumper's West Indian takeaway, and asked if I wanted to make a few shillings. I couldn't say no. He regarded selling bush on the Frontline as a dangerous pastime. He operated from various addresses in the Brixton area. He'd pick me up in his two-liter Rover and order me to "keep a good watch for any dutty Babylon." He'd sell to his selective clients by appointment (most of them white people). He sold an ounce of weed for £40. Hash was cheaper. He'd order me to buy a hundred small polythene bags (used for buttons) from a local dry cleaner.

He imported a barrel of cannabis a month direct from Jamaica. I had no idea how he navigated that amount through customs. He owned a white van which had building materials, tools, and dark blue overalls inside. An ax sat below the driver's seat. Clipping wads of ten- and twenty-pound notes under his pressed slacks, he'd disappear for two or three days and return with a new barrel. He never revealed from which port of entry he made the pickup. Sometimes he'd ask me to go through the ounce bags, take out all the seeds, and snip off the stalks with a small pair of scissors. I'd get high simply breathing in the aroma. He didn't smoke and warned me, "Those tings give yuh cancer, mon."

The crime lord said, "Me want ah good reputation. That's why the white mon come to me. Me nah sell no mixed herbs or fuckery weed. Ah pure collie weed me ah deal wid. This stalk of sinsemilla *direct* from Jamaica."

For my labor I was paid £5 a morning or afternoon.

He disappeared following the 1981 Brixton uprising. Whispers reached me that he had been murdered in Jamaica. His body had apparently been tossed into a gulley near Kingston. Nothing was ever confirmed. Nunchaks, the Brixton crime lord in *East of Acre Lane,* was based on this individual.

"Me 'ave ah liccle business in Handswort' to attend to," *Nunchaks announced. "I should be back by de end ah nex'* *week. An' when I reach, if me don't see de t'ings dat you*

t'iefed, I'm gonna personally peel your fingers like raw carrot wid my machete, to raatid. Y'hear me, yout'?"

Of course, I spent whatever I earned in Soferno B's record shack, and if I had any change, I'd buy myself a beef patty or a cheese-and-bun snack from Tumper's store (I was a regular customer even though Tumper never offered me a discount on my lean days).

The gangster I worked for wasn't wrong that retailing weed on the Frontline could be a dangerous occupation. I'd been witness to several stabbings and carvings. It was usually a dispute between rival weed hustlers or a "lineman" showing off his hard-earned reputation. Toxic masculinity. The slightest hint of weakness or fear was preyed upon. You had to lift your head, push out your chest, step with confidence, and show hard Brixtonian eyes.

On one occasion I spotted an unfamiliar face bouncing up Railton Road trying to sell his cannabis wares. He was threatened with a meat cleaver, ordered to peel off his gold rings, his Cecil Gee cardigan, and his lizard-skin shoes. Whatever weed he had was taken from him. He was dispatched to the Brixton tube station wearing only his socks, slacks, white stringed vest, and a traumatized expression.

When I reflect on the time I spent at the Frontline, there is always one song that enters my head: Dennis Brown's "I Don't Want to Be No General." Backed by the murderous rhythm section of Sly Dunbar and Robbie Shakespeare, Dennis Brown addressed the top rankings directly: *I don't want to be no general, to end up in a funeral . . .*

He warned: *The top rankings all get a spanking . . .*

In my experience, the above is certainly true.

NEW TRAINEE

....

In the fall of 1979, I managed to catch my social worker at his office on Herne Hill Road. I requested a handout, explaining that I had no food at home. Before he presented me with a five-pound note to buy groceries, he asked how I was getting on.

I shrugged.

He wanted to know about my interests.

I explained that I loved reggae music and sound systems. I said that one day I was going to build my own sound system with my bredren Valentine, and it'd be the best in South London, if not the world.

"Are you interested in carpentry?" he asked.

"Not really," I replied.

"But building speaker boxes involves carpentry, doesn't it?"

"I s'pose so."

"Excellent!"

Before I knew it, my social worker had arranged an interview with Lambeth Borough Construction Services on Porden Road, next door to Brixton Town Hall. I left that office with a new status—a trainee carpenter for Lambeth Council. With my new wages, I was encouraged by my employers to buy a tool a week to build my collection.

A tool a week? I wanna buy music!

I was based at the maintenance depot on Lingham Street, Stockwell. I caught the 50 bus to work. My duties were to observe skilled carpenters going about their business fixing and repairing broken window frames, doors, kitchen cupboards, staircases, windowsills, floorboards, fences, signposts, and on one occasion a rabbit hutch.

The job bored me from the outset. I spent most of my time lugging around a heavy carpenter's tool bag all over Lambeth. "Me glad you're wid me, Alex," a Jamaican carpenter admitted to me once. "You save me ah money. Me don't have to jump 'pon ah bus wid me tool bag to reach any appointment."

"Why don't you give me half of the bus fare you're saving yourself?" I suggested.

"Don't get feisty, Alex!"

I wanted to build double-bass speaker boxes (which Valentine referred to as *cows)* or at least work on a construction site where I could learn how to build something from the ground up. Instead, I found myself hanging fire doors on the fifteenth or sixteenth floor in a tower block. The lifts always seemed to fail as I offloaded timber from a Lambeth Council pickup truck.

With my current lifestyle (which involved arriving home at five or six in the morning from parties and raves at least three times a week), I found myself searching for excuses why I couldn't make it to work on any particular day. Life on the street was simply too exciting, the reggae music too enticing.

Following five months or so of my constant nonattendance, Lambeth Council fired me. My social worker threw up his hands in the air and said, "No more handouts!"

"But you're responsible for me," I protested.

"Not if you keep throwing away job opportunities."

Youth unemployment was very high in Brixton in the late

'70s and early '80s, though a few friends of mine did manage to hold down jobs. They'd come to visit us at Elm Park, and they would rage at how their bosses treated them. They cited racist language, constant insults, and if they complained, they were told they had a chip on their shoulder, that they couldn't take a joke.

We'd share a spliff and a drink with them. We'd blow weed smoke up their nostrils, and before you knew it, they'd be late for work the next morning.

There is always a reggae track apt for any situation. Gregory Isaacs's "Poor and Clean" perfectly spoke of our frustration. Backed by the rhythm twins Sly Dunbar and Robbie Shakespeare, Gregory's line, *No one knew my pain, Lord, yet I would pay the cost*, resonated deeply within me.

I admit that I made some bad choices in my young life, but as Gregory said, no one understood the constant pain I was tormented by. Sometimes I would simply wake up angry and never fully understood where the fury came from.

I didn't want to admit that I was suffering from trauma. I tried to stop my mind from bringing up incidents from my childhood. I'd shut my eyes and turn up the bass of whatever track I was listening to. Quite often, it was a futile attempt to drown out whatever my core wanted to express.

Even when I was asleep, my agony and loneliness were awake. Miss Joyce Cook appeared in my dreams. She was a giant with King Kong–sized fists. I was tiny. There was no escaping her belts, fire pokers, and wooden hairbrushes.

I'd wake in a cold sweat and wrap another spliff.

There was one small problem Valentine and I had to overcome before we could achieve our dream of owning a sound system.

Money—or in Brixtonian slang, *corn*.

We needed eighteen-inch Goodmans bass speakers, mid-range and tweeter box speakers, a 500-watt valve amplifier, a customized pre-amplifier, a record deck, and other accessories.

Joining us in our ambition to conquer the world were Croydon and Thornton Heath bredren Andrew Lawson, Royston Muirhead, and Winston Taylor. (Winston already owned an impressive reggae collection.)

We decided to build the bass speaker boxes first. For our material, we visited building sites and timber yards at night in the Croydon area. There were always sheets of three-quarter-inch chipboard and plywood lying around. If we found a box of two-inch screws, that was a bonus.

Whenever we spotted approaching headlights, we would set the sheets flat on the ground and lie on top of them.

In Valentine's back garden, we constructed our "houses of joy."

"No nails are gonna be used in our speaker boxes," Valentine insisted. "It has to be two-inch screws. So Papa Cass teach me so!"

We'd heard of a loudspeaker warehouse/store somewhere near the Crystal Palace football stadium, so Valentine and I decided to pay it a nighttime visit. Protecting the back of the store was a two-meter meshed fence. Valentine and I easily negotiated it. There were dog patrol signs, but we ignored them.

The building had a skylight and we reckoned that would be our point of entry—back doors were usually alarmed. We were armed with screwdrivers, pliers, and hacksaws to snap any catch or lock. We shinnied up the drainpipe and carefully crawled along the angled roof—a section of it was meshed glass. We reached the skylight and easily opened it. I switched on my flashlight as Valentine prepared to climb down.

He was halfway through with his feet dangling near

the floor when we suddenly heard this demonic barking. I pointed the light to the ground but couldn't locate the hound. From its deep tone, I could tell this was no corgi. Valentine screamed, "Help me up, Wheats! Help me up!"

I pulled him up, then we scrambled along the roof, jumped to the ground, and somersaulted the fence.

I teased Valentine mercilessly about the dog, sometimes creeping up on him and barking in his ear.

"Wheats, it's not funny! I hate dogs."

As a writer, I simply could not allow that experience to go to waste, so I employed it for a humorous scene in my novel *East of Acre Lane*.

We returned to the loudspeaker store, this time as paying customers. We had pooled our money and bought our first eighteen-inch (it *had* to be eighteen-inch) Goodmans bass speaker. We bolted it onto our single speaker box and padded it out (so it wouldn't vibrate) with roof insulation material that we had borrowed from a nearby building site (that stuff gave me a thousand itches).

Papa Cass had taught us well.

We didn't have our 500-watt valve amplifier yet, but we did own a 100-watt transistor amplifier. The speaker box was hauled up to Valentine's bedroom (his mum monitoring us so we wouldn't scrape the walls). We connected the necessary wires and jack plugs. Satisfied, we sat there in nervous anticipation.

Valentine decided to play his favorite track of the day, L. Jones's "Daydreaming of Africa." Andrew's fingers caressed the bass knob. The flute intro kicked in above a solid one-drop reggae beat. The bass dropped. *Wow!* An unforgettable moment as we felt the breeze from the speaker box vent.

"We're official," Valentine declared. "Yes, the official Crucial Rocker sound system is now in session."

"Turn it down!" Valentine's mother cried. "You're shaking up the place! Me nuh want the ceiling to drop 'pon me!"

We all exchanged wide smiles.

Valentine closed the door and urged Andrew to crank up the bass. The cussing from downstairs was the most colorful I have ever heard.

As I left Valentine's home that evening, a neighbor walked up to me and asked if I was helping Valentine's family with building work.

UNMERRY CHRISTMAS

....

From as far back as I can remember, I detested the festive period. It wasn't created for sufferahs like me. Even now as I write this, I hate the commercialization of it all. It's the worst time of the year for lonely people.

Back in Holly House, during the buildup to Christmas, I would always be on paper-chain duties. I'd spend hours licking and linking the decorations before they were taped all around the dining room, hallway, and lounge. Balloons and cards were put up too. The Christmas tree (a real one) was placed in the lounge where fairy lights were twisted around it and presents from children's relatives were set beneath it.

On Christmas morning, Miss Joyce Cook would refuse to unlock the lounge door until every child had finished their breakfast. If I had my way, I would have remained in bed all day.

Once allowed into the "sitting room," I had to watch other children open their presents from various relations and try to match their joy as they blessed their eyes on new footballs, matchbox car racing tracks, action men, space-hoppers, chopper bikes, a Subbuteo table football game, *Monopoly* and *Escape from Colditz* board games, roller skates, Tiny Tears dolls, pop albums, or soccer annuals. (Days later, I would benefit from any football-related books and gifts when they were discarded.) Also, one child always received the *The Guinness Book of World Records*.

The only aspect of Christmas Day I enjoyed as a child was the serving of fizzy drinks at dinnertime. Coca-Cola, Tizer, cream soda, lemonade, the choice was ours. Mine was always cream soda.

With the household, I'd watch the queen's speech and then a film. I remember going for a kick-about with one of the older boys in my cottage, Kevin Donnelly. He played center forward for his school, and for a Sunday football club called Spring Park Wolves. Every Christmas, one of his relatives bought him a new pair of soccer boots or a football. His certificates graced the mantelpiece in the dining room.

He'd take me up to one of the two football pitches we had within the grounds of Shirley Oaks, put me in goal, and he'd practice his shooting until dark. My fingers stung at my attempts to save the ball, but I'd rather fetch a wayward shot from the sharp nettles than sit in Holly House on Christmas Day.

I'd spend Christmas Day evening sitting on my bed in my dormitory rereading the comics I had collected. I'd wonder who my parents were, what they looked like, where they might be living. *Are they eating turkey, roast potatoes, brussels sprouts, and Yorkshire pudding?* I'd close my eyes and create my own siblings. Of course, they'd be film stars, famous singers, and soccer players. I'd imagine the world's greatest footballer of the day, Pelé, coming to claim me as his lost son. I'd dream Diana Ross was my mother. She'd serenade me with the other Supremes. They'd buy me my own Christmas tree. All the presents beneath it would have my name written on the tag. They'd place tinsel around my bed on Christmas Eve night.

My stocking would be big enough for the giant in *Jack and the Beanstalk* and I'd have enough chocolate to rival whatever they had in Willy Wonka's factory.

Loneliness attacked me mercilessly at Christmas, and 1979 was no different.

I was alone in the hostel. I fried myself corned beef and boiled Uncle Ben's rice. I sat in my bedroom watching *Dr. No* on a grainy black-and-white TV. After James Bond saved the world, I ventured out to the Brixton streets and peered through front windows. I tried to imagine what a family Christmas was like. I tried to comprehend what having a brother, sister, aunt, uncle might mean.

This experience seeded the creation of Brenton Brown, the lead character in my debut novel, *Brixton Rock*.

> It was cold in the room on this December night; Christmas was just around the corner. Brenton was visited by a sudden sense of isolation and bitterness. He wondered whether he had any brothers or sisters; maybe an aunt or uncle; then his mind rewound to his childhood spent in a children's home. He recalled the Christmas period when the more fortunate kids would spend the holidays with their families . . .

That Christmas in 1979, I returned to my hostel distressed and reached for my Bob Marley collection. To lift my spirits, I played "Three Little Birds" from the *Exodus* album. I sang along with the lyrics as tears fell down my cheeks. *Every little thing is gonna be all right* . . .

Again, I cursed God.

I remember one time when I was a child attending a

church service, the priest informing the congregation that the meek will inherit the earth and God recognizes the pain and tribulation we all endure. "He will never forsake you and will reward you in heaven."

Dear reader, forgive me if this sounds blasphemous, but in my bouts of depression during the festive period of 1979, I concluded that preachers' promises were a whole heap of fuckery.

I willed the day to finish as quickly as possible. Following my meal, I smoked as much weed as I could manage and slept until Boxing Day.

REGGAE TEMPLES

In the early 1980s, there were plenty venues in South London and beyond where you could listen to the top-ranking sound systems of the day. In the Croydon area, there were Friday nights at the Parchmore Youth Club, the Rainbow all-nighter in East Croydon, and St. Alban's Church hall just a few minutes' walk from Selhurst Park, the home of the Crystal Palace football club.

To ensure a ram-jam crowd, local sound systems, including Ital Rebel, Natty Combination, the Mighty Observer, and Jah Rocker, would often invite popular sound systems from the Brixton area.

One great day in early 1980, Soferno B accepted the Mighty Observer's invitation. Flyers were printed advertising the event, slacks were pressed, Afros were flicked out, shoes were polished, dresses were dry-cleaned, and hats and berets were adjusted.

One of my new Brixton friends, Floyd Windett, had access to his mother's car: a white Datsun with tinted windows. "Don't even breathe on the bodywork," Floyd warned. "And fling your spliff butts out the window!" (Someday I might pen that white Datsun's autobiography—it could tell a tale or two.)

We all piled in for the drive to Thornton Heath.

The queue to gain entrance was long, and the men on the gate growled like mercenaries in a never-ending war. It was a corked affair. Every reggae-head from a five-mile radius was present. Big Yout', Soferno B's DJ, was spinning some dangerous tunes and the Mighty Observer was soon told to "sign off." Because Soferno B were so popular with the crowd, that meant they selected every single track from that point on. It was embarrassing for Observer, but at least they could look forward to their share of the gate money.

At least Rhino, the skanker, enjoyed himself, charging to all corners of the place.

At the conclusion, my bredren were happy to bank girls' telephone numbers in their back pockets.

Stuck in heavy traffic, trying to turn right onto Parchmore Road, we spotted three girls walking home from the dance. My friends dared me to get out of the car and chat with them. I was threatened eviction if I didn't comply. I hadn't picked up any girl's number during the evening—shyness still crippled me.

Nervously, I climbed out of the car. The young lady I approached was very pretty, with sultry eyes. "Did . . . did you go to the dance?" I managed.

I was embarrassed by roars and chants from the car. "Gwaan, Wheats! Don't tell her any fuckery! Don't leave without the digits!"

I caught the young beauty's gaze and asked for her name.

"Maureen," she replied with a smile.

Before I knew it, she had written down her phone number. I pushed it deep inside the back pocket of my Farah slacks. *Yesssssss!*

Arriving back at Elm Park, I was given a celebratory spliff for my achievement. (I declined the Special Brews and Tennent's.)

I rang Maureen the next day but quickly put down the phone when her father picked up.

Eventually, I managed to speak to her. I discovered that Maureen liked soul music too, and her favorite reggae artist was Barrington Levy. That was more than good enough for me.

I'd had stoned fumbles and liaisons with other girls. One reggae-head young lady I knew would sneak me into her house after her churchgoing parents retired to bed. I'd creep upstairs to her bedroom where I'd stay until five a.m. When I'd hit the street, I'd have to wait for the first number 50 bus to reach home. I still don't know how we managed to get away with it. Truth was, many West Indian parents were rather conservative; my generation had to be creative.

Maureen was the first girl I properly dated.

I'd visit her at her home opposite the Thornton Heath and Streatham cricket grounds. The front room was brightly decorated. I'd study the family photographs on the mantelpiece and the framed portraits on the walls. I'd wonder what the interior of my own mother's home looked like. There was a Jamaican calendar stuck up in the kitchen. Seasoned chicken attacked my nostrils.

Maureen's mother was incredibly welcoming to me, often serving me a West Indian dinner, but her father looked at me as if I were a great pestilence. When he was home, he'd never allow us to spend too long alone in the lounge—ten minutes was the maximum.

For Maureen's birthday, I bought her a Barrington Levy album, *Robin Hood.* My fave Barrington track has always been "Bounty Hunter." *Mr. Hunter man, you're hunting, you're hunting all over this land . . .*

Valentine and I watched Barrington Levy and Linval Thompson perform at a *Black Echoes* magazine award show.

"Bounty Hunter" tore down the house that night. He sounded just as good live as he did on vinyl.

Being with Maureen gave me so much confidence; finally someone genuinely cared for me and wanted to be with me. Maureen and I dated for a few months, attending parties, blues dances, and sound system clashes. Every time I hear a Barrington Levy track, I think of her.

CRUCIAL ROCKER FORWARD

· ·

Crucial Rocker sound system's debut performance was at Valentine's older sister's flat in Shrublands, a small council estate wedged between Addington, West Wickham, and Shirley. I can't claim it was a ram-jam affair. Not too many reggae-heads lived in Shrublands, and it was a bit of a trek from central Croydon and Thornton Heath. The last 194b bus left before eleven p.m.

Our speakers and amplifiers worked well though. Nothing exploded, which was a relief. (I've seen several smoking valve amplifiers in my time.)

At Shrublands, it was the first time I ever picked up a microphone. Not because I had a burning desire to become a toaster, but it had been left unemployed on top of the pre-amplifier. I picked it up and introduced the tracks and artists. I unleashed my inner U-Roy: "*And now we have the mighty Dennis Brown 'pon the turntable. Tune call 'Money in My Pocket,' so you'd better skank like you never skank before and don't bother stand up against the wall and be a bore. By the flick of my musical wrist, I play reggae music that you can't resist! So tek a sip and shake your musical hip! All night long sweet reggae music ah go drip! Sound call Crucial . . . Rocker!*"

At the end of the night/early morning, Valentine informed me, "Okay, Wheats, you're the mic man of our sound. Don't fuck it up. You better think of a name for yourself."

I thought about it. Alex-Roy didn't quite work. Nor did A-Roy, U-Wheats, or Daddy Wheatley. I'd spent a lot of time building speaker boxes in Valentine's backyard, so I settled on Yardman Irie.

I wasn't aware of it at the time, but words were my thing. From five or six years old, I took such great comfort in reading comics like *The Beano*. I wanted to create my own comic strip. At the same time, I read the sports pages and articles at the back of the newspapers. For Crucial Rocker I had to invent rhymes, jingles, and lyrics as Yardman Irie. Several years later, in my early twenties, I became a spoken word poet known as the Brixtonbard. For me, it's all part of the same journey: the need to tell a story.

Our next dance was on Alexandra Road in Addiscombe, Croydon. Valentine had an uncle who lived there, and the uncle figured he could make some change if he bought drinks at the cash-and-carry and sold them in his kitchen at inflated prices while Crucial Rocker played the music. We'd make our money at the door. It was a blues all-nighter. The venue was close enough for the Thornton Heath, Norbury, and South Norwood reggae-heads to trod to.

We considered ourselves a professional outfit, so we printed tickets to advertise and handed out most of them to girls at the Sir Philip Game Centre. We believed that if we could persuade the females to attend our dance, the guys would follow. We weren't wrong.

Ravers started arriving before eleven p.m.—a good sign. By half midnight, the place was corked. Mr. Dyer, Valentine's uncle (he looked sharp in his royal-blue three-piece suit, fedora, and black brogues), was well happy. "Announce on the mic that all drink is available at the bar," he said. "We have brandy, whiskey, and white rum!"

The entrance fee was £1. Royston manned the door. Valentine and Winston selected, Andrew was at the controls, and I was the MC. "*It's I, Yardman Irie, at the microphone stand, with the champion sound system inna Croydon land. So find yourself a liccle corner, we play reggae music hot like a sauna, and dance 'pon your toe, Crucial Rocker will mek it flow.*" It was pure bliss to hear the crowd chant "Rewind" and "Pull up" whenever we played a satisfying tune.

Just after one a.m. we heard a commotion at the front door and all went to investigate.

A Thornton Heath badman didn't want to pay his fee, so Royston had denied him entry. "Do you know who me is?" the guy threatened. "Do you know me raasclaat name?" He pulled out a blade. It shined under the streetlight. "Don't fuck wid me!"

We stood firm at the door.

A standoff.

Side-eyes and glares were exchanged.

It was one of the longest minutes of my life.

"Your sound wort'less anyway," said the knifeman. He kissed his teeth, snapped shut his blade, and drove away at high speed in his Cortina Mark II.

We went back inside, and the next tune Valentine selected was Gregory's "Soon Forward." Backed by Sly and Robbie, the vocals are just sublime as they glide over a hypnotic one-drop rhythm. The song is in my all-time Gregory top three. *Soon forward, come turn me on . . . Turn your lights down low now . . .*

We all pulled a girl to crub with. "Rewind, selector!" We played sweet reggae music and danced away until morning peeked through the windows.

We collected over £130 at the door. Mr. Dyer made over £200 at his bar and quickly booked us for a once-a-month residence.

All profits were put back into the sound system. We built more speaker boxes, bought new reggae releases, and updated our pre-amplifier. We also placed a baseball bat and a cricket bat inside the record box for protection in case anything kicked off.

Quite often, I made the trip to Daddy Kool's reggae record store on Dean Street, in Soho, where in their basement they sold revival records stretching back to the 1960s. They had original copies of Treasure Isle– and Studio One–produced 7" records. I spent hours flicking through collections by the Heptones, the Techniques, the Paragons, Slim Smith, Ken Boothe, Hortense Ellis, Marcia Griffiths, Jimmy Cliff, Desmond Dekker, the Skatalites, the Pioneers, the Wailers, Toots and the Maytals, and so many more.

The owner of the store was a white reggae-head called Keith. What he didn't know about reggae wasn't worth speaking about.

I built another record box to house my revival collection. It was bloody heavy!

FINDING IDENTITY

....

I constantly felt apprehensive being invited into my friends' homes.

Valentine's mother was particularly welcoming. She always cooked a big pot of food and encouraged me to *fill ya belly*. At her table was where I first tasted West Indian food. Her soup with yams, dasheen, green banana, dumplings, and stewed beef was a delight on a cold day. The only soup I had tasted previously was minestrone or tomato.

It took me awhile to understand her thick Jamaican patois, but I'll forever remember her kindness and compassion. She had lost her husband when Valentine was very young, and raised him and his sisters on her own. It must have been incredibly difficult. Despite her loss, she always managed to serve a hot meal in the evening. She kept a clean house. Family photographs stood proud in her immaculate front room. Valentine never went hungry, nor did he want for clothes or anything else.

I was nervous in her presence because I didn't want her or anyone else to question me about my own family. At this point in my life, I simply didn't know the circumstances of my birth or why I was placed into care. Whenever Valentine's family discussed this uncle or that aunt living in the Caribbean, I would shy away to a corner of the room, staring at the floor and hoping I wouldn't be interrogated about my own background.

Even when I was among my own friends, I felt massive embarrassment whenever they discussed their parents or grandparents. With pride, they'd say their mum hailed from Spanish Town, Maypen, Port Maria, or their father was born in Negril, Port Antonio, or Kingston 11.

I had a map of Jamaica taped to one of my favorite reggae albums, *Right Time* by the Mighty Diamonds. For long periods, I stared at this map and whispered to myself the names of all the towns: *Montego Bay, Mandeville, St. Anne's Bay, Ocho Rios, Browns Town, Oracabessa.*

I'd often walk to the phone box on Brixton Hill that stood outside Brixton prison. I'd thumb through the *W* section of the phone lists. I'd stop at *Wheatle* and circle the details with a pencil. There were addresses under that surname in Tottenham and Tulse Hill. I'd pick up the receiver and wonder who'd be on the end of the line if I dialed the number. I'd place it down in a panic. I was tempted to knock on their doors and ask if they knew any member of my family. I'd sleep on it, wake in the morning, and decide against it. What would I do if I called on a white family who happened to share the Wheatle name? It could prove very embarrassing. I didn't even know my father's first name. I imagined them calling the police on me, claiming that I was scouting a property to burgle at night.

I wondered where my parents were born and raised. For all I knew, it could have been St. Vincent, Grenada, Trinidad, or St. Lucia. I tried to imagine what they did for a living and if they cooked the same dishes as Valentine's mother.

A similar scenario played out when I was introduced to

relatives of my Brixton friends. I was continually asked, "Your parents Jamaican?"

I hoped they were, because of my love for Jamaican music and culture, but I couldn't answer yes with any confidence.

"Your friend too quiet," they would comment. "Him lost him tongue? Where him come from? Him sound too English. Him strange!"

I'd try to escape any family gathering at the first opportunity, often excusing myself because I had to wash my clothes or perform some other errand. I'd retreat to my bedroom in the hostel and play reggae music to uplift myself.

The Mighty Diamonds's "Identity" really captured my sense of loneliness: *We're running around like a lonely sheep . . .*

Late one night, I stood on the platform of the Brixton underground station as the headlights of the onrushing train filled the tunnel. I heard the rattling of the live rail. I closed my eyes and prepared to leap. I sucked in a long breath. *No one gives a fuck about me,* I said to myself. *Who the fuck's gonna be at my funeral? No fucking one! Fuck everyone! Fuck this life.*

I'm not sure why I stepped back as the tube train whooshed by me. The wind cooled my cheeks. I rocked back on my heels. My heart raced.

I walked slowly back to Elm Park, sat on my bed, and meditated for what seemed like hours: *Where did we lose our identity?*

Years later, I used that near-fatal experience to inform my character Brenton Brown. For me, it made sense that Brenton would have his final confrontation with Terry Flynn on the Brixton underground platform. It was a live-or-die scene. My narratives are categorized as fiction, but each one is informed by a lived reality.

PARTY HUNTERS

....

Follow the bass line, we used to say in Elm Park if we didn't have a late-night dance to attend on a Friday or Saturday evening (we branded ourselves the Elm Park Internationals). Finding a rave was never a problem because Brixton was reggae-head heaven.

Reggae was played on pirate radio stations, hi-fis and "Brixton suitcases" on every street corner, tower block balcony, barbershop, hair salon, domino club, building site, launderette, park, garage, market stall, Brixton Town Hall, and on one memorable morning, the employment exchange (someone decided to entertain disillusioned job-seekers with a cassette tape full of Dennis Brown).

Where I lived was quite central, just half a mile or so up from Brixton Town Hall. On a quiet Sunday morning I could hear its clock chime.

We'd trod up to the New Park Road and Palace Road council estates that ran parallel to the South Circular Road. If we couldn't gain entry at a private party, we'd step into the nearby Tulse Hill Estate or check out the streets leading off Brixton Hill. If unsuccessful, we'd step to the Poynders Road Estate off Kings Avenue. West of Acre Lane was the Notre Dame council blocks which hosted a blues party now and again. On the odd weekend, we'd venture farther north into the Stockwell Park, Stockwell Gardens Estate, Angel Town, Loughborough, Myatts Field, Cowley, Black Prince Road, and Dorset Road urban jungles. We never failed to find a bass line vibrating in one corner or other of South London.

Of course, we'd keep a lookout for cruising SPG police vans. It simply depended on their mood if they decided to raid a dance or not.

The entrance fee was usually a pound, but if you carried a bottle of Pink Lady, Captain Morgan, Bacardi, Thunderbird, or four cans of Special Brew beer, the gateman would sometimes allow you in. (Quite often, he'd grab the drink for himself to stash in his car.)

I witnessed desperate reggae-heads taking a hammer to the metal money container of red phone boxes. They'd arrive at the blues dance with 2p coins. The doorman counted every penny. Pretty girls only had to flash a smile at the gatekeeper for free admission. "Yes, sister! You're looking seriously scrumptious!" the gateman would flirt with a smile. "Come in, gal! Come in! We'll dance ah liccle later!"

"Can I get a freeness?" a rough-looking sufferah would ask.

"Freeness!" the gateman would roar. "Tek your serious body odor to the bridge where you sleep under!"

If the sound system had yet to build a reputation or a following, we'd send in a scout to the dance, and he had to provide a forensic report on the number of girls in the venue.

"It's dry, mon! Not ah single female in sight. Let's step."

"The gal dem coming later," the gateman would insist.

"Later in your dreams!"

If it was man-heavy, we'd kiss our teeth and move on until we heard the next bass line.

The top party/blues dance sound systems in Brixton included Soferno B (who had a weekly residence in Villa Road), Sir Lloyd, Studio One, Frontline International, and Dread Diamonds. We didn't have to send in any kind of reconnaissance for their sessions. It was advisable to reach their dances early (around eleven p.m.) and find a spot near a window (for ventilation purposes). By the end of the night or early morning, you were a few pounds lighter because of the sweat expended. A few brothers I knew carried a change of shirt, deodorant, and "trodder" boots inside their "sticksman" bags.

Early morning light would reveal the bruised wallpaper from all the serious crubbing that occurred.

At Villa Road, Soferno B would board up the windows with black-painted chip and plyboard. Reggae-heads would pay their fee at the door up until six in the morning. They'd rave until noon Sunday. Girls left straight to church after washing off their makeup in the bathroom.

Seeing a throng of Black reggae-heads waiting outside a cab office, white minicab drivers would refuse to pick them up. (I must admit that on more than one occasion, when the taxi driver reached my destination, I opened the passenger door and bolted.)

Don Carlos's classic "Nice Time (Late Night Blues)" pays homage to all-night reggae raves: *We're gonna love this music tonight, we're gonna have nice time tonight . . .* Robbie Shakespeare's bass line is one of the most pulsating and dangerous ever committed to a reggae record. Mixed by Prince Jammy at King Tubby's quarter tower, it literally blew me away.

While writing this book, the great Robbie Shakespeare passed away on December 8, 2021. He was simply a colossus of reggae music on the bass guitar. I can't even begin to count how many classic hits he contributed to. Hundreds, if not thousands. A true legend. May he rest in eternal reggae peace.

EXPLOITATION

....

To alleviate mass unemployment in the early 1980s, especially among young people, the government introduced the Youth Opportunities Programme (YOP) where an employer, funded by the government, trained a young person at their place of business for six months, preparing them for future employment that would lead to a secure job.

The pay was £23 per week, a few pounds more than a fortnightly unemployment check. With traveling expenses, those few pounds more turned into a few shillings.

A friend who lived with me at 15, Elm Park, decided to take on a position at a clothing shop in the West End of London. During his six-month stint, he never missed a day (unlike me). He thrived in customer relations, performed every task required of him, smiled his best smile, bought his own slacks and shirts for work, and was regularly informed that if he worked hard, there would be a permanent role for him at the store.

When the six months concluded, he was released by the shop. He discovered a week later that they had taken on another young person on the same YOP scheme. My bredren cursed some serious badword. I wrapped him a long spliff so he could calm down.

Blatant exploitation.

When I was unemployed, I'd trod down to the employment exchange on Brixton's Coldharbour Lane. Job vacancies were displayed on laminated cards fixed on boards. There were always positions for chambermaids, cleaners, road sweepers, and laborers. You picked a job description and handed it to an employment advisor over a counter (they always looked as miserable as a cold beggar in Toronto).

With my carpentry knowledge, I searched for work on building sites. Sometimes I found a one- or two-day shift mixing cement, carrying bricks, making mugs of tea, or cleaning up the workplace. A broom spent more time in my hands than a saw. I'd inform my employers that I could insert locks, hang doors, fit windowsills, cupboards, and frames. They'd laugh at me and say they wouldn't want to risk me performing expensive skilled work.

"Where's your credentials?"

I didn't blame them. I had had an opportunity at the Lambeth Council construction services and fucked it up.

However, the cash-in-hand building site work that I didn't declare to the employment exchange kept me in reggae vinyl, imitation silk flower shirts, and Jamaican patties and chips.

But there were also jobs that I absolutely hated.

Next door to the employment exchange was an industrial laundry. They cleaned the bedsheets, linen, and towels of West End hotels. I lasted three days before a foreman yelled at me, "Stop being a lazy African and get those fucking sheets in the basket!"

I told him to fuck himself hard with his bottle of Coke.

I think I did four shifts at a McDonald's in Clapham Junction before I was presented with a blue jacket, a black rubbish bag, and told to pick up any McDonald's litter on the street.

"They got road sweepers to do that fuckery," was my response.

"When employees start with us," my boss explained, "everyone is expected to perform this task. It's sort of a ritual."

"Well, I ain't doing it," I said. "Fuck you. Put *yourself* in the fucking bag."

I did eventually train as a center lathe turner. I studied for six months at an engineering skill center in Perivale, West London. "We're going to train you to machine components to a thousandth of an inch," the instructor informed trainees on the first day.

A thousandth of an inch? I said to myself. *Is that possible?*

It was.

The commute from South London was horrible, but I managed to gain a qualification and a living from the trade for many years.

Stepping through Brixton's Granville Arcade in the fall of 1980, I discovered a new reggae record shack—the General record store. It was only about thirty steps away from Soferno B's.

I was fast approaching eighteen years old. Shopkeepers and reggae-heads now recognized me. They nodded to me in the streets as I passed by in a semi-swagger. I had perfected my strut. I could understand Jamaican patois and Brixtonian slang. I was becoming more confident with every passing day. I now considered myself a ripe Brixtonian.

"Hey, Wheats!" a bredren called out to me. "Where are you stepping wid your t'ree-quarter trousers and your imitation chops (fake gold bracelet)? No fit gyal is ever gonna grine you."

"And no A-class gyal is gonna grine *you* wid your dry hair

that needs to step to a petrol station to slap nuff oil on it and your crusty cheeks that's demanding a serious dose of cocoa butter!" I'd reply.

"Wheats! You t'ink you ah Brixtonian now?"

"Yes, bredren, more Brixtonian than the foundations of the town hall, to raatid!"

"You still the living bumpkin from the land of Oz!"

"And you're still a cruff wid no gyal!"

I moved on to the General record store.

Behind the counter was Chinese-Jamaican George, a bubbly, likable character who had a knowledge of reggae that was unrivaled. Whenever I coched in his store, we debated many topics, such as the amount of weed you get in a two-pound draw, the latest news of local crime lords, what bad boy was on the run, updates from recent sound system sessions, raids by the police on the Frontline, the latest sufferah to be kicked out by his parents because he grew dreadlocks, and the current liberation struggle in Zimbabwe.

George was a founding member of the Nasty Rocker sound system that boasted Ricky Ranking and Lorna G as their resident DJs/toasters. Years later, Lorna established herself as a fine actress, appearing in West End shows and television dramas including the *Small Axe* series. She also had a hit with a song titled "Brixton Rock."

I'll never forget the first tune George played for me: "Saturday Night Jamboree" by Wayne Jarrett and Silver Fox. Customers banged their fists on the counter and hollered their approval: "Rewind! Rewind! Rewind!" Mixed by Scientist at King Tubby's quarter tower, the track was a favorite at any dancehall I stepped to.

Whenever I had enough money for travel, I'd take a trip to Peckings Records just off Uxbridge Road in West London. They stocked exclusive Studio One releases direct from Jamaica.

Occasionally, I'd drop by Daddy Kool in the West End to search their basement treasure trove for rare revival tunes.

As my record collection grew, I dreamed about running my own pirate radio station.

PART II
BABYLON SYSTEM IS THE VAMPIRE

NEW CROSS FIRE

....

When I headed home from a blues dance or party in Brixton, I was sometimes mocked by reggae-heads cruising by in their Cortina Mark IIs, Triumph Dolomites, and Ford Capris. "Trodder!" they would yell in my direction. "Do you want a lift?" they would shout, before pressing down on the accelerator. I believe this prank was inspired by a scene in *Saturday Night Fever*. Laughter would trail in their slipstream.

Occasionally, the teasing as I walked home would take a more sinister turn. "Nigger!" a white guy would scream as he sped by with his mates in a Volkswagen Beetle or a Mini.

It was all part of my weekend experience in the late 1970s and early 1980s. At least I always made it home. Some were not so fortunate.

I learned about the New Cross Fire when I was in Soferno B's record shack on the Monday morning following the tragedy. A Brixton lineman said, "White mon fling firebomb inna de yard. De place ketch ah fire. Nuff sufferah dead. Me gwaan wet up de neck of ah racist white mon tonight. See if me don't! Bloodclaat devil people dem!"

A forlorn shadow marked the faces of every reggae-head I saw that day. That initial sadness quickly turned into anger.

The New Cross Fire occurred on January 18, 1981, at a birthday party for two teenage girls. I had recently turned eighteen myself.

"Wheats! You're now old enough for the beast to keep you and beat you inna cell for more than twenty-four hours," a bredren warned. "Mind where you step. Resist any arrest. Don't let the beast corner you inna cell."

Everyone was convinced the New Cross Fire catastrophe was a racist attack. Many of us had been subjected to racist abuse in school, our places of work, on the streets, and by the police.

Prior to the tragedy, the nearby Moonshot Centre youth club, which many young Black people attended, mysteriously went up in flames. The Albany arts center, a hub for young Black creatives, suffered the same fate.

Black New Cross and Lewisham felt under attack.

Every reggae-head knew that it could have been any one of them who had lost their life. Many of us believed it was the police who launched a firebomb into the house.

Before I had reached the age of eighteen, I had been beaten up by the police twice and racially insulted by officers more times than I can remember. As far as I was concerned, they were more than capable of such a despicable act.

The Black People's Day of Action march, scheduled for March 2, 1981, was a protest against the unsatisfactory police investigation into the fire. I couldn't join the start of the demonstration in Deptford because I had a job interview that morning (I wasn't successful), and after that I jumped on a 109 bus to Waterloo.

I heard the rally near Blackfriars Bridge before I joined it.

I was astonished. An endless mass of Black faces made its way toward the bridge. Banners held aloft. Afros, dreadlocks, weatherman caps, and tams. *Thirteen dead, nothing said!* they chanted as one. I have never felt as empowered as I did on that day. I hardly recognized any of the people around me, but a surge of Black pride and belonging filled me. I raised my fist and offered my voice: *Thirteen dead, nothing said!*

It was clear the police didn't want us to cross the bridge. Someone spoke through a loudspeaker and said the route had already been arranged with the authorities. I felt the Black tsunami behind me. It ebbed forever forward. They didn't have enough numbers to hold us back. In their desperation, they attacked protesters at the front of the rally. Batons drawn and fists clenched, they lashed out. We fought back with interest. Running battles ensued. Panic stamped their expressions; we broke through their ranks.

Halfway across the bridge I was rugby-tackled to the ground. As I wriggled and threw a punch to free myself, a fellow protester came to my assistance and kicked the officer off my back. We exchanged knowing smiles. *He who feels it knows it.*

"The niggers are in the city," a policeman barked into his radio. "There are millions of 'em!"

Racist abuse was also hurled down from upstairs offices: "Why don't you fuck off back to your jungle!"

"Why don't you get your white bombaclaat raas down here and say that to my face?" a sufferah shot back.

The invitation wasn't accepted.

"You don't belong here!"

Monkey chants followed.

The situation was incredibly tense.

March stewards attempted to calm our responses to the racial abuse.

I started to fret about my chances of making it back home

to Brixton. *The Brixton police are brutal, city beast might be worse.* There was safety in numbers. *Stay with the march, Alex,* I told myself.

"Why aren't there more police to control the coons?" someone called from above.

At times, it was hard not to react, race into an office block, smash a window, and wreak vengeance.

Linton Kwesi Johnson's "New Crass Massahkah" perfectly summarized the New Cross Fire in compelling dub poetry: *Physically scarred, the mentally marred . . .* I had already become aware of LKJ from "Sonny's Lettah," where he relates the story of a young Black man's arrest.

On the evening of March 2, 1981, when I made it safely back to Brixton, something had changed. I could see it in the faces of fellow sufferahs who rode the bus with me.

Yes, we can stand firm and put up resistance. If there will be blood, then mek it run. We're more than ready.

ARRESTED DEVELOPMENT

....

Soon after the Black People's Day of Action, the police response was to introduce their "Swamp" initiative where they clamped down on street crime in the Brixton area.

They flooded the streets with more officers and employed the hated "SUS" law. It felt like a military occupation. They stopped Black people with impunity. They didn't need a reason—they justified their actions by claiming we looked like we were about to commit a crime.

In two days, I was stopped and searched three times. On the first occasion, I was walking home from a blues dance around six in the morning when a "beast wagon" screeched in front of me. They informed me that I fit the description of a suspected burglar.

"And you fit the description of a racist pig!"

"I don't think this one got his manners from his Black mammy."

"Fuck you and the ugly trog that gave birth to you!"

Even though I carried no bag, I was forced to lie flat on the ground as they handcuffed me and emptied my pockets. They confiscated my Afro comb stating it was a weapon, and stole the change I had in my pocket, but they failed to seize the small bag of weed I had slipped in my left sock (all my bredren did this).

"What are you doing out on the streets so early?" one of them challenged. "Looking out for old dears to rob?"

I cut my eyes at them and kept silent.

On the second occasion, I had just emerged from the unemployment exchange on Coldharbour Lane and was about to go coch in Soferno B's record shack. Once again, they claimed that I fit the description of a criminal. This time a mugger.

"They haven't got the balls to mug any of *us*," one of the cops said. "They go for little old ladies."

I didn't want to be humiliated lying facedown on the street again, so I raised my hands. "I ain't got nothing. Go and search if you have to, but I'm gonna holler out if you plant any shit on me."

As they checked my pockets and my body, I whispered, "Dutty Babylon." I know they heard me, but I'm not sure they understood my meaning.

Three hours later, I was admiring gold rings through a glass window of a local jewelers. Of course, I had no funds to buy any bling. Before I knew it, the same officers who had stopped me outside the unemployment exchange pulled on my arm and ordered me to raise my hands.

"Thinking of running in there and nicking some gold, eh? You nonstick bitches love a bit of gold, don't you?"

"And we love fucking your women too," I snapped back. "And they love it! You wanna hear their moans?"

They tried to force me to the ground and secure handcuffs to my wrists. I put up resistance and kicked one officer in his chest. I managed to free myself and made my getaway up Atlantic Road. I headed onto Barnwell Road and then kicked onto Brixton Water Lane. I checked behind me and they were no longer in pursuit.

From that point onward, I kept my wits about me.

"Don't let the beast arrest you, Alex," a hustling bredren advised me. "It'll be sufferation inna cell."

In the first two weeks of March 1981, friends reported police raiding blues dances, getting arrested for carrying a bag of plumbing tools, being searched and humiliated in a nightclub queue, and being intimidated at night by slow-cruising SPG vans.

One bredren of mine who lived on Mayall Road, which ran parallel to Railton Road, had his front door rammed off its hinges, his lounge and bedrooms trashed, floorboards ripped up, windows smashed, his hi-fi kicked to the floor, and his reggae collection stamped on.

They found two small bags of weed (he had an ounce buried in the garden). He was arrested and spent the night in a police cell.

The tension mounted. They were now our sworn enemy. Many of my elders spoke of Olive Morris and how we must revive her spirit.

Olive Morris was the seventeen-year-old heroine who intervened when police assaulted a Nigerian man on Atlantic Road in 1968. For her involvement, she was arrested, driven to the Brixton police station, savagely beaten up in a police cell, and threatened with rape. When her family eventually arrived to claim her, they could barely recognize her under her injuries.

A seventeen-year-old girl.

For many Brixtonians, the burning injustice of what happened to Olive will never be forgotten.

In 1986, Lambeth Council decided to name one of its redbrick office buildings on Brixton Hill in honor of Olive Morris.

* * *

If we suspected anybody of assisting the police, or liaising with them, they were immediately rejected and forever labeled a "beast informer." They were refused entry to any dance and often "draped" of any money or valuables they carried.

We decided that if the police confronted us again, we'd put up resistance and refuse arrest. We weren't willing to accept any more indignities.

The truth was, I and so many others were ready for war. I could never rid my mind of the hollering and wailing from big Trevor, owner of King Solomon Sound, who had been next door to my cell in the Brixton police station and suffered that vicious beating. I could not forget the ordeal of waiting in my cell for my own beating. And yet, back in the late '70s and early '80s, nobody would describe what I had witnessed and endured as trauma.

Still, a day of reckoning would come.

LIVE AND DIRECT FROM ELM PARK, BRIXTON HILL

....

My fellow budding toasters and I tried to imitate our DJ heroes from Jamaica in my room at Elm Park. We'd set up two boom boxes: one to record and the other to play an instrumental version of a hit reggae song.

"Pass the Kouchie," later adapted by the UK teen group Musical Youth into a number one British single, "Pass the Dutchie," was a massive underground reggae hit. When you hit the dancehall, DJs from the top-ranking sound systems, including Sister Nancy, Brigadier Jerry, Papa San, and Yellowman, queued up to "chat" over it.

My Elm Park sessions were meant to be a spontaneous freestyling affair.

But I cheated.

My limited skill set denied me creating lyrics on demand. I couldn't freestyle to save my TDK cassette tapes. Before my bredren arrived one evening, I had scribbled something down and rehearsed for a couple of days or so.

There were four of us prepared to wage lyrical warfare: Papa Crooks, Elfego Barker, Remington Moses, and myself, aka the Private Yardman Irie. We all wore our berets, weatherman hats, and nine-carat gold (in my case gold-plated).

Egos swelled, spliffs were lit, Special Brews and Tennent's were drained, the bass was set to max, and someone pressed record.

The horn intro to the instrumental kicked in. I closed my eyes, pulled mightily on my big head, exhaled through my nose, and, inspired by Sister Nancy, I began:

To you
This one is dedicated to you
Elfego love to drink nuff cans of Special Brew
When you go to his yard I beg you don't use the loo
The stench from the bowl could kill an elephant too
When Moses burn two spliffs he don't have a clue
He starts to bounce around like a mad kangaroo
Him walk so strange you think him do a doo-doo
Papa Crooks will never date the pretty gal Sue
Him don't believe it but my words are true
When him last chat to her the gal start spew
The fit gal Janine live on Kings Avenue
Her love for me is well overdue
When she go ah dance she always wear blue
Me chat two nice words but she cold like an igloo
When sweetboy go ah dance he wears his reptile shoe
When you crub nice gal, stick to her like glue
Me always come with lyrics that are brand spanking new
Me always stand firm against the boys in blue
Me don't like to see tiger caged inna zoo
To step to Sir Lloyd dance you must join the long queue
Me lyrics so hot you must send for the fire crew
It's I Yardman Irie so bouncer let me pass through
Over the nest the cuckoo did flew
My girlfriend calls me her big coo-ca-choo

She cooks me stewed chicken, rice, and callaloo
If you fuck wid me I'll take out my nunchakoo
I'm more rapid than Bruce Lee, take that for true . . .

"Forward, Yardman Irie!" everyone chanted. "Forward!"

Good gosh! If only camera phones and social media were available back in the early 1980s.

The reputations of the top-ranking South London sound systems spread far and wide. Reggae-heads from Bedford, Birmingham, Leicester, Aylesbury, Leeds, Manchester, Nottingham, Cardiff, and many other West Indian enclaves in the UK wanted to experience hard-core reggae music *direct* from Jamaica and floor-rumbling bass lines from a stack of eighteen-inch speakers.

If you spent most of your free time in Soferno B's record shack like I did, opportunities presented themselves.

One Friday afternoon, Big Yout' arrived at the reggae store to recruit "box boys" for a trip to High Wycombe. I had never heard of the town before and had no idea how far out of London it was.

I raised my hand. "I'll go."

"Check me outside the shop tomorrow at four thirty p.m. Don't be late."

"I'm there already!" I replied.

The next day, I met the van half an hour early.

Big Yout' and his selectors filled the front seats. Box boys traveled in the back with the equipment. Our duties were to lift and carry the valve amplifier, cables, amp casings, and speakers into the venue. When the session concluded, we had to bring everything back just as we had found it.

"If you drop anyting," Big Yout' warned, "you drop ya life!"

Including me, there were six box boys in total.

I found myself perched on a "cow" as the shutters were pulled down. Only lighters, lit matches, and burning spliffs pricked the darkness. (We were also responsible for any equipment damaged or burned en route.)

We pulled away. I'm not sure how long the journey took, but I suffered a bruise as the van braked sharply and a mid-range speaker box rammed my back.

When we carried the boxes into the hall, a crowd had already assembled. Rastafarians wore their tams, women sported their head wraps, and stepper boys practiced their moves. The man who'd booked the sound greeted Big Yout' as if he were a visiting monarch. "You reach!" he exclaimed. "T'ank the Lord, you reach! Me start fret! Is there anything I can do?"

"Yeah, mon," Big Yout' growled, "where the weed?"

"I'll get you a draw."

"And the liquor," Big Yout' requested.

Us box boys were treated like royal aides.

Not trusting anyone else to carry the pre-amp, Big Yout' informed us that in towns like High Wycombe, they were starved of reggae music. They didn't have any official radio program, nor were there any reggae record shacks around to coch in.

We went to work under the watchful gaze of onlookers. We connected the speaker boxes to the valve amplifier and secured the overhead wires to the ceiling and around door-frames with masking tape. Dozens surrounded the control tower where Big Yout' applied his final checks.

Finally, Big Yout' switched on the pre-amp. When he turned on the record deck, the hall rapidly filled.

"Where did all those reggae-heads come from?"

Later, we discovered that ravers had driven for more than forty miles to catch the session.

Big Yout' wiped the needle and grabbed the microphone. *"In tune to the A1, hit-bound greatest sound system inna the universe, Soferno B!"*

The audience roared. Whistles were blown. Fists were raised.

The first record of the night was Dennis Brown's "Cup of Tea"—one of my faves. *Pass the bread around . . .*

The crowd went nuts. I had never seen reggae-heads skank so hard on the first tune they heard. *A fish for you and a fish for me, a break of bread and a cup of tea . . .*

I danced for an hour or so before fatigue claimed me. Big Yout' had arranged a fish-and-chip supper. At the end of the night, he paid me and the other box boys five pounds each for our labor.

On the return journey to London, a tweeter box dropped on a fellow box boy's head.

"Me hope your headtop didn't damage the tweeter box," Big Yout' remarked later. Risk assessment wasn't a thing in sound system culture.

We arrived back at Villa Road just after two a.m., but there was already another session to prepare for—a blues dance.

While Big Yout' and his selectors went home to shower and change (Big Yout' took his pre-amp with him), my fellow box boys and I had to carry the gear into the house and "string up" once again.

By the time I had finished my work, I was too tired to enjoy the session despite the presence of so many women inside the venue. I decided to rest in the van.

"Wheats! Wake up, mon!" another box boy called to me.

"There's nuff girl inna the dance. Yuh nuh waan crub wid any of dem? Wake up!"

"I'm too mash-up," I protested.

"You're missing out. The music sweet too."

BRIXTON UPRISING

....

Friday, April 10, 1981

It was an unusually warm spring day. To cool off in the evening, a few of my bredren and I played pool in the George the Fourth pub on Brixton Hill opposite the Brixton prison.

As I nursed a pint of shandy for over an hour or so, I won most of my games. My friends were getting pissed off because the winner didn't have to punch his "sheckles" into the pool table to release the balls to start another match.

Sometime after nine p.m., a Black boy of about thirteen or fourteen years of age burst into the establishment. Shock spread from his eyes. "Dutty Babylon just wet up a sufferah!" he announced. "Him dead for true!"

The world paused.

I don't think any of my bredren questioned the words of the teenager. We all knew from experience what the police were capable of. An image of Trevor gate-crashed my mind.

We rolled out of the pub and headed down Brixton Hill. Sirens could be heard in the distance. Flashes of blue lit up the night sky over central Brixton. An SPG van chased another vehicle into Brixton Water Lane. Tension hung in the air.

A Black woman stood outside the launderette on Brixton

Hill and peered down the road. "Babylon kill ah yout' 'pon de Frontline," she said. "War is coming fe real."

We visited a friend who lived on the fifth floor of a block in the St. Matthews estate which ran parallel to Brixton Hill. "Yes," he confirmed, "beastman wet up ah yout' 'pon de Frontline. Him dead. Whole heap of sufferah want dem revenge. They fling brick and boccle after the beast dem. Big tribulation coming to Brixton."

From what we understood, a young Black male had just left the games arcade on the Frontline and had an altercation with a police officer. Somehow, it resulted in the stabbing of this young brother. Apparently, the officer even blocked an attempt from onlookers to take the sufferah to the hospital. Police reinforcements were called, and when they arrived, they were attacked with bricks and bottles. A delegation of community leaders was on its way to the Brixton police station to try to convince the local commander to scale down the police presence in central Brixton.

They were dismissed.

The situation was volatile.

We wanted to score our usual Friday-night weed on the Frontline, but we decided against it as Railton Road was hot with beast activity. SPG vans cruised through the main arteries of Brixton.

We trod to the flat of a herbalist who lived in Tulse Hill estate. As we bought five-pound draws of Jamaican collie, he told us, "The radication squad murdered a yout' 'pon de Frontline. Everybody talkin' 'bout war. Be careful where you linger at nighttime. The beast could kill you next. They will tell the judge it was self-defense."

We stopped by a friend's girlfriend's house in the Palace Road estate, just off the South Circular Road, to drop off her five-pound draw. To satisfy our inevitable munchies, she cooked us fried dumplings and baked beans. Spliffs were lit, reggae was played, and reasonings began.

A consensus was agreed that we had to make a stand.

When I arrived home after three a.m., police sirens still rang out in the warm Brixton night. I tried to stay awake for as long as I could because I didn't want to miss anything.

Saturday, April 11

My usual coch on a Saturday morning was listening to reggae music in Soferno B's record shack. *Do I dare to step down there later?*

That night/early morning, I remember playing a Freddie McGregor cassette tape: *We need more love in the ghetto . . .*

I fell asleep in my clothes with a half-smoked joint dangling from my mouth. I woke up with a burned bottom lip.

For my breakfast the next morning, I fried an egg and placed it on a slice of bread. I chased it down with water.

I headed for central Brixton just after ten a.m. I noticed that the streets were unusually full of young Black people for that time of day. The police presence was evident too. They walked in twos and threes. We side-eyed and snarled at them and they returned our glares. Traders and shopkeepers swapped nervous glances as they sold their wares. Their voices were not as urgent as usual. Even the tramps, the confused, and the idlers appeared a little wary.

The white bare-backed dreadlocked dancer who usually skanked beside a music stall near the entrance of the shopping arcade was missing. There was a long queue at the West Indian bread shop. Shoppers' eyes continually flicked toward the streets. The number 2 bus driver looked apprehensive as he inched his way through the traffic down Atlantic Road.

I took up my usual spot in Soferno B's record shack. Johnny Osbourne was the hot artist of the day—anything the guys behind the counter played with Johnny singing on it sold like cool spring water in a desert.

The shop slowly filled. The windows vibrated to the cranked-up bass line. Flyers of reggae dances and blues parties were picked up and discussed. Sound systems were praised and trashed.

"Welton Yout' is the best DJ inna Brixton!"

"No, mon! Tippa Irie!"

"Champion better than all of dem."

"No, mon! General Slater the top-ranking mic man inna Brixton."

"What about Dego Ranking?"

"Nobody ah talk about Marshally."

I went out to buy my lunchtime chicken patty just after noon. I decided to walk around the market. The fish smelled as good as it always did. Customers haggled for the best deals. Vagrants begged for change outside the Brixton tube station as was their custom. Desmond's Hip City, another West Indian music store, won a healthy stream of business. (They catered more to the musical tastes of my parents' generation.)

The barber saloon opposite Soferno B's was packed with sweet boys, already prepping for the night's raving ahead. The staff in the Baron's menswear store were happy to receive a constant flow of customers who bought their reptile-skin shoes and belts, Farah slacks, imitation silk shirts, and Gabicci cardigans. A sign in their shop window said a request for credit would be politely refused.

I made it back to Soferno B's where they played another Johnny Osbourne track. *Folly ranking, you're 'bout to get a spanking*. Hands went up in the air. Fists slapped the counter. Skankers danced. *Oh what a shame, what a big disgrace . . .*

Suddenly, outside, a wave of people ran toward the junction of Atlantic Road and Coldharbour Lane. The shop emptied, 7" and 12" records were left on the counter.

I followed the flock.

When I arrived at the scene, I could barely believe my eyes. A police van had been tipped over onto its side, the bodywork caved in, the windshield and windows smashed.

"Dutty Babylon!" someone screamed.

Four police officers ran for their lives down Atlantic Road. One of them had a gashed forehead, another had left his helmet behind. Sufferahs were already making their way toward Railton Road to prepare a barricade. Upstairs windows were opened. One of them had a poster of Che Guevara stuck to it. Sirens screamed from every direction. Mothers grabbed their kids off the streets. Pensioners pulled their shopping trolleys as quickly as they could manage. A lady paused as she was about to pay a vendor for her apples. Shop-front shutters slammed down. Drinkers in the Atlantic pub came out wondering what the hell was going on. A guy emerged from the barber saloon with half his head trimmed. Two young brothers who had been in the queue for the West Indian bread shop joined the crowd that gathered on the Frontline.

Pure adrenaline flooded my arteries. In the back of my mind, I knew what my fate would be if I ended up in a police cell. I thought of Trevor and raced to join the throng.

I was ready.

Low brick walls fronting terraced properties were hacked down with crowbars, metal mallets, hammers, and brute force. Milk and fizzy drink bottles were assembled. Dustbins were emptied out onto the road. Barriers erected. Petrol was drained from cars and then they were tipped onto their sides to fortify the barricade.

"When they come, stand firm!" someone hollered. "Nuh let dem pass!"

We didn't have long to wait.

To this day, I'm not sure why a lone police vehicle drove up Railton Road to confront us. Maybe it had gotten lost and wasn't aware of the precarious situation?

When it was spotted, the sky darkened. An assortment of missiles filled the air: bricks, bottles, plant pots, tin cans, jam jars, a biscuit tin, spanners, tobacco tins, hammers, cabbages, frozen fish, dustbin lids, and what looked like the head of a tailor's dummy.

Whoever drove that police Allegro must have felt like hell was chasing him. He reversed at top speed, almost running over a pedestrian.

There was a short lull in the battle as everyone tried to process what they had just witnessed. I glanced behind me. There must have been hundreds of sufferahs waiting for the war on the Frontline to kick off.

About fifty yards down the road, scores of police were employing dustbin lids as shields to protect themselves from the missiles that rained toward them. They tried to advance in an ordered line.

We kicked down more low walls and tore down corrugated fencing that covered the windows of squats and derelict housing.

I noticed rioters preparing Molotov cocktails to launch into the massed police ranks. As I peered upward, everything seemed to be orange. The street was a carpet of glass shards, debris, petrol, burning cars, and broken bricks. I searched the faces around me. The determination to hold and stand firm on the Frontline was clear.

As the afternoon and early evening progressed, the heat from the burning cars and Molotov cocktails stung my eyes. The temperature rose significantly when the George pub, standing at the junction of Effra Parade and Railton Road, was set alight. The establishment had a long history of refusing to serve Black customers (my father included, I later discovered).

It was one of those moments I will never forget as the flames raged through that building and kissed the warm night sky. The walls blackened and crumbled. The window frames collapsed. The glass splintered. There was this awful crunching sound. I felt the tremor beneath my soles. No fire engine could get near it without being attacked.

"Babylon is burning!" someone screamed.

My arms were almost spent from the constant throwing, but someone informed me that the beasts were attempting to catch us by surprise from behind. They were moving down the Herne Hill end of Mayall Road, a route that ran parallel to Railton Road.

About sixty of us, armed with all the bricks and missiles we could carry, ran to meet them. We turned left onto Shakespeare Road, and we quickly decided to employ a tactic that had proven successful for us earlier in the day: fifty or so would remain hidden in back gardens or "friendly" houses and about a dozen of us would engage the police, throwing our missiles into their positions and then luring them into an ambush. I was one of those who formed the "carrot," for I was a swift runner.

Thirteen of us marched up Mayall Road, knowing the rest of our group was lying low in two terraced houses. All lights were switched off. We spotted the police about a hundred yards away and all that lay between us were several busted, smoking cars.

At this point—I'll never forget it—from somewhere above, a reggae-head played Max Romeo's "Melt Away." *A smoke has been driven to drive them away.* The haunting bass line seemed to drift on the smoke. *As wax melt before the fire, so shall they melt away . . .*

It felt surreal, like we were in our own movie. *He who sits in the heaven shall laugh, for Jah shall have them in derision . . .*

As soon as the police were in range, we hurled all and sundry into the air. They immediately charged at us. Feeling great fear and excitement, we turned on our heels and ran for our sweet reggae lives. Again, I was only too aware of what might lie in wait in a police cell.

As we sprinted by the junction of Chaucer Road and Mayall Road, the police were caught in our trap. One revolutionary had even climbed on top of a house to better launch his missiles. But a few of the police carried on chasing. With panic coursing through my veins, I scorched left onto Chaucer while the rest of my guerrilla group dashed down Mayall. To my alarm, five policemen were still in pursuit. As I approached the perimeter fence of Brockwell Park, I considered trying to clamber over the barrier and into the darkness. But my arms were too tired. I had to rely on my speed of foot. I kept running onto Brixton Water Lane, almost tripping over myself.

Still they hunted me.

Turning left onto Tulse Hill, I made for the nearest council estate I could find. My heart raced ferociously and as I glanced back, the police had yet to turn the corner from Brixton Water Lane. Upon entering the estate, without thought or hesitation I leaped into one of those gray metal council rubbish bins. I was exhausted and just had to rest. I tried to control my breathing. I fretted because I didn't have my asthma inhaler with me.

The stench emitting from the black garbage bags meant little to me. There I remained for half an hour, not daring to peep over the bin wall. Sweat dripped down my face.

Fearful of police snatch squads driving up and down Tulse Hill, Brixton Hill, and Acre Lane, I made my way to my hostel off Brixton Hill via the back streets. Once inside, I drank greedily from the cold tap in the kitchen. Then I took a quick bath. Getting dressed, I noticed my hostel mates had been busy looting. There were new clothes everywhere, alongside boxes of cigarettes and bottles and cans of liquor. The fridge was full of Special Brew, Tennent's, Heineken, and Skol beer. Downing a Coca-Cola, I tried on a new pair of slacks—they fit perfectly.

Being a sound system DJ known by the moniker of Yardman Irie, I wanted to write a new song, or at least start one. I managed the chorus and four lines:

Uprising, this an uprising!
Uprising, this an uprising!
Uprising, this an uprising!
We're sick and tired of the ghetto housing
And the damn SUS law and police beating
We have no work and we have no shilling
We can't take no more of this suffering

Months later, when I was released from prison, I finished the song:

So we gwaan riot inna Brixton and inna Sout'all

We gwaan riot inna Parliament and inna White'all
You better send for the army and the Home Guard
We gwaan mash up and burn down New Scotland Yard
Come listen, sufferah, to the Brixtonbard
Police officer, you better put up your guard
Uprising, this an uprising!
Uprising, this an uprising!
Uprising, this an uprising!
We get up in the morning at ten thirty
Forward down the hill to Brixton city
And sight Babylon dem start attack we
And we start fling stone and masonry
Police officer get lick in dem belly
And the temperature raise by another degree
While nuff sufferah start a looting spree
Uprising, this an uprising!
Uprising, this an uprising!
Uprising, this an uprising!

Wanting to recapture that adrenaline rush, I made my way to central Brixton again, via the back streets. I noticed that in the council estates, people peered over their balconies. Militant reggae music boomed out of every street and, despite the police cordoning off Brixton from Streatham Hill and Kennington, packs of young sufferahs poured in from all avenues, wanting to be part of the uprising. There seemed to be a thousand alarms ringing out in the night.

One siren sounded from a hi-fi shop situated on the corner of New Park Road and Brixton Hill. By the time I reached it, the windows had been blitzed and everything was gone. Not even a single jack plug remained.

I realized that the looters were targeting the off-licenses, preparing for the inevitable parties and blues dances. From New Park Road to Hayter Road, not a single shop-front window was spared. Even the pharmacy was hit. Every other step I felt the crunch of broken glass.

Smarties, Marathon bars, Milky Ways, Mars bars, Kit Kats, Tic Tacs, Trebor mints, Fruit Pastilles, gum, crisp packets, cigarette papers, magazines, newspapers, cheap lighters, cash registers, nappies, flu remedies, milk of magnesia bottles, bandages, toothbrushes, boot polish, and anything else that I have forgotten littered the streets.

Returning to Railton Road via Brockwell Park, I noticed that the police had gained relative control of the Frontline. They were housed in numerous green coaches, sipping hot drinks from polystyrene cups. Fear was written over their faces. They looked like they'd rather be at home, nursing a beer while watching *Match of the Day*. It was an empowering sight to behold. Sudden movements by police on the ground informed me that rioters were still throwing missiles.

Tumper, the proprietor of the twenty-four-hour West Indian food and takeaway store on Railton Road (his premises were untouched by the rioters), did a roaring trade selling fried dumplings, cheese-and-bun sandwiches, carrot cake, and fish fritters. Queuing up to buy a snack, I bumped into a hustler friend of mine.

"Dey took a raasclaat beating, innit," he said.

"Yeah, they did." Quoting Max Romeo's "Melt Away," I added, "*Batter, batter, batter dem to pieces.*"

My bredren laughed.

Melt away, like ice cream, scream, scream, scream . . .

AFTERMATH

....

I finally hit my pillow at some point after five a.m.

I couldn't sleep because my body was still charged with adrenaline. It seemed that the entire London police force was abroad in Brixton. Every now and again a blue light flashed by my window. I thought at any moment they'd bust down my front door again and haul me away to the police station for another booting in the ribs.

I watched the dawn roll in through my bedroom window.

I ate two Mars Bars for my breakfast and chased it down with Coca-Cola. *Why didn't somebody loot a box of eggs and a couple of sausages?* I thought to myself. *Or even a bag of flour so I can fry some dumplings.*

I went upstairs to the lounge and discovered five or six bodies sleeping on sofas and armchairs. The floor was full of looted clothes, shoeboxes, sweets wrappers, empty drink cans, and ashtrays brimming with cigarette and spliff butts. I found new clothes left in my wardrobe from friends who didn't want their parents to discover that they had been looting.

"Don't even think about pulling on my new slacks, Wheats!"

* * *

I made my way down Brixton Hill.

Shopkeepers stared at their properties in total despair. One woman swept the glass and debris away from her premises and remarked, "At least they never burn it down."

There was a massive police presence—they had cordoned off all of central Brixton. The closest I could reach was St. Matthew's Church opposite the town hall. Unanswered alarm calls rang out from all directions. Distant shouts were heard. The smell of petrol and smoke hung in the air, mingling with the tension.

Sufferahs showed off their new clothes, shoes, and jewelry, a few even complained that their new shirt or jacket didn't quite fit. They openly smoked their "big heads." Hustlers tried to sell packets of cigarettes at reduced prices. Packs of cigarette papers went for 2p. If you wanted liquor, you could follow them back to their yard where they had untold crates.

Again, the police glared at us and we scowled back at them. For the first time since I had moved to Brixton, I was no longer scared of the beast. Fear had rebounded back on them.

I returned home with an extra bounce in my step and slept until the next day.

Monday, April 13

A loud banging on the front door woke me up just after nine thirty a.m. Believing it was the police, I quickly dressed, pulled back my net curtain, and checked along the street.

It was a bredren at the door, and he didn't look too happy. I let him in and he complained that he couldn't cash his unemployment check because the post office was closed. He also grumbled that he had missed the uprising because he was out of town visiting relatives. His third gripe was that the parents of his girlfriend had forbidden her from visiting him as they were frightened for her being out and about in Brixton.

I fell about in hysterics.

He cussed me for not being sympathetic. "I haven't had sex for three weeks!"

We shared a breakfast of Twix bars and creme eggs before we lit spliffs, drained Coca-Colas with a splash of rum, and discussed the uprising. I slotted a Dennis Brown cassette into my Brixton suitcase. We nodded heads and got well charged.

My bredren departed in a better mood.

If I was pushed to name my all-time favorite reggae artist, it would have to be the crown prince, Dennis Brown. He was such a consistently great songwriter, and while the world had Bob Marley, we sufferahs felt that Dennis belonged exclusively to us.

When I reflect on the uprising, the soundtrack in my mind is dominated by Dennis Brown's "Revolution," one of his greatest songs: *Are you ready to stand up and fight the right revolution?*

Three years later, on July 7, 1984, I watched Dennis perform "Revolution" at the Reggae Sunsplash concert at Selhurst Park. The audience erupted. Many in the crowd exchanged knowing smiles, believing Dennis was referring to the 1981 Brixton uprising.

"A riot is the language of the unheard," said Dr. Martin Luther King Jr.

He wasn't wrong.

BABYLON STRIKES BACK

....

Reggae-heads in Brixton and all over the world mourned the passing of Bob Marley on May 11, 1981. As we rolled into June, I still found it difficult to accept the death of the king of reggae. I had never experienced a family loss, and this felt so personal. His music was played everywhere in those sad days.

Many of my fellow sufferahs had lost faith that our lives would ever improve, or that we would ever escape Babylon, the Western society that still chained us in poverty and plagued us with racism.

We reflected on the legend's words:

Ah I and I build the cabin
Ah I and I plant the corn
Didn't my people before me
Slave for this country . . .

Several Rastafarians I knew postponed their plans to migrate to Shashamane Land, a region in Ethiopia. Ever since I had arrived in Brixton, they'd spoken of the milk and honey to be found there.

"Yes, mon, the Black mon doesn't belong in Babylon," a

Rasta elder preached to me at the Twelve Tribes of Israel settlement in Kennington one evening. "Why do we toil under the white mon's yoke? Africa for Africans, home and abroad. So Marcus Garvey said it. Red for the blood the white man spilled from our ancestors, green for our homeland, and gold for the sun that blessed our backs."

"Bob Marley never reach there," someone said. "Babylon kill him!"

"Cancer kill Bob," another Rasta argued.

"Babylon give him cancer!"

"The white mon blood dat flow t'rough Bob give him cancer."

"Him shoulda cut off him big toe."

"We must look for ourselves to win liberty," said an elder. "We cyan't rely 'pon one mon."

"We will never taste total liberty in Babylon."

"Africa must be free by 1983!"

I was instructed to read the prophecies of Marcus Garvey, who said to look to Africa for leadership and guidance. They recommended the Mighty Diamonds's classic *Right Time* album (I had already bought it). They schooled me in recent Ethiopian history. A Black emperor, Haile Selassie, had been crowned on April 2, 1930. He was the King of Kings and the Lord of Lords, direct descendant of King Solomon and the Queen of Sheba. He didn't bow to anyone. His nation had defeated fascist Italy in the 1930s.

The belief and sense of purpose that the dreads had was severely tested by the passing of Marley, the "Tuff Gong."

"You must keep the faith," pleaded another elder. "Natty dread nuh give up."

Meanwhile, despite uprisings in Toxteth, Handsworth, Moss Side, and many other concrete jungles in the UK,

---

Prince Charles prepared to marry Lady Diana Spencer. I had next to no interest. They may as well have been a couple of aliens tying the knot on Mars.

To celebrate, street parties were planned all over the UK, even in Brixton. Sufferahs on the Frontline organized a festival, but it wasn't to mark Prince Charles and Diana's wedding. They proposed to host a reggae concert/dance in the children's adventure playground on the Frontline on the day of the wedding. They sent out invitations to Ranking Joe, one of Jamaica's top MCs, and Leroy "Horsemouth" Wallace, one of Jamaica's top reggae session drummers and star of the film *Rockers*.

Sir Coxsone provided the sound system. Reggae-heads from all over London and beyond planned to attend.

I never made it to the concert. I remember switching on my radio in the early morning: Smokey Robinson's "Being with You" trilled from the speakers.

Then I heard an almighty crash.

The front door had been flattened. Heavy boots stomped the hallway. It didn't take much effort for the police to force open my bedroom door. I didn't even have enough time to pull on my jeans as four or five officers came for me. I lashed out with my fists and kicked with my feet, but I was soon overpowered. They handcuffed me and bundled me outside. They launched me into the back of a police van and I hit the floor with a solid thud. My ribs vibrated. (Coffin Head's arrest in *East of Acre Lane* isn't fiction.)

"Did you think you'd get away with it, nigger? Did you?"

Once again, as I lay on the van's floor, I felt every bump, pothole, and ramp as they sped down Brixton Hill. I sniffed the aroma of a thousand arrests.

They arrived at the police station and opened the back

doors of the vehicle. My shoulders were bruised and I refused to step outside. "I ain't going nowhere, you fucking dutty piece of white shit! Take your hands off me, you pagan swine!"

I was still only dressed in my briefs.

An officer tossed me my jeans and T-shirt. "Put them on, midnight!"

It wasn't easy tugging on a pair of pants while handcuffed.

Following a scuffle, they yanked my feet and I crashed to the ground, splitting open my forehead.

"I don't wanna be infected with *that*," an officer commented. "He might have rabies."

Stunned and bewildered, I was dragged and presented to the charging officer. I was charged with assaulting a police officer, resisting arrest, and causing property damage.

They hauled me downstairs, my feet barely touching the steps, and they shoved me inside a cell. Trevor's vicious assault played back in my mind on a continuous loop.

When are they gonna come for me? Why don't they beat me now and get it over and done with?

I closed my eyes and hummed a tune: *Six Babylon attack three dreadlocks, just ah lock them up cos they're smoking a spliff . . .*

I can't remember how many hours I sat in that police cell. I can't recollect speaking to a duty solicitor. All I can recall is that I promised myself that if a single officer dared to enter my space, I would kill them. If I served a long stretch, then at least it would be for a crime I willingly committed. *Fuck them!*

Sometime later, they served me food that I refused to even look at.

They released me after ten p.m. I must have spent well over twelve hours at the police station. I was summoned to appear at the Camberwell Green magistrates' court the following Monday. I was disorientated. Hungry. Thirsty. Bitter.

Left and a right, Babylon on the ground
Left and a right, natty dread on the ground
Babylon, cool down your temper, sa . . .

When I arrived home, I spotted someone fixing the front door. I entered my bedroom and found that my boom box and several of my records had been smashed. Shattered glass covered the floor. One of my notepads was ripped to pieces. If I'd had the energy, I would've hot-stepped down to central Brixton and thrown a petrol bomb into the police station. *Babylon have to burn.*

Instead, I collapsed onto my bed. Thoughts coursed through my head about running away. *Where will I go? Maybe the Addington Hills? I can make some sort of camp, steal some food, and hide out for the rest of the summer.* I knew the area well. *If it rains, maybe I can bust into someone's shed and kip there. The beast might stop hunting for me come October. Perhaps I can live at a bredren's yard? Yeah, just keep a low profile. Wait a minute—I don't want any bredren's house getting mash-up by the beast if they come hunting for me. If there are any dreads still planning to make an exodus to Shashamane Land, maybe I can tag along with them.*

The following few days were a blur. Loneliness and depression hit me with a vengeance. This kept me from sleep. Miss Joyce Cook loomed large in my mind. Fire pokers, wooden hairbrushes, soiled bedsheets, shovels. *Your parents left you on the dock of the bay. You're nothing. You should be grateful we provided food and shelter.*

I didn't want to be sober anymore. I smoked as much weed as I could manage and afford. When the high subsided,

I had to confront the fact that I was completely alone in this world. I had nobody to call a mother, father, sister, brother, or even cousin.

Twice, I stepped down to the Brixton tube station. There, late at night, I sat with my back against the wall and my eyes closed. I tried to summon the courage to fling myself in front of an onrushing train.

"Are you all right, love?" I remember a white woman asking me. She regarded me kindly. Compassion twinkled in her eyes.

I didn't respond.

I can't recollect many details about my court appearance. A bredren offered me a white shirt and tie to wear. I was asked to stand in front of the magistrate before he passed judgment. I glanced at the public gallery. There were several Black people there. Mums, dads, aunts, and maybe uncles. It occurred to me that if my own parents were sitting there, I wouldn't even recognize them. How pathetic was that? A sense of utter rejection overwhelmed me. *No one gives a flying fuck about you, Alex Wheatle. No one!*

My knees buckled and I had to reach out to the barrier in front of me to keep myself upright.

I received a nine-month sentence. It might as well have been ninety years.

They led me down to the cells. Linval Thompson's words echoed inside my head: *Babylon, cool down your temper, sa.*

AT YOUR MAJESTY'S PLEASURE

Sometime after six p.m. I was ushered to a prison van. It had individual cubicles inside and darkened windows. There was little room to stand up or stretch my legs.

First stop was a secure holding facility near Lambeth Walk. There, new prisoners were dispersed all over the UK. My next destination was the Wormwood Scrubs prison in West London. On the journey, I wondered what new tunes played in Soferno B's record shack. I'd miss the lively banter and all the new Johnny Osbourne, Wailing Souls, Dennis Brown, Linval Thompson, and Barrington Levy releases. *Will I ever attend another reggae dance or blues party again?*

Protected by barbed wire, the high walls of Wormwood Scrubs came into view. I heard the back door of the van being opened and was led out into a compound with a dozen or so others. No one said anything.

We were taken inside. Bob Marley's "Burnin' and Lootin'" played inside my head: *This morning I woke up in a curfew . . .*

I was ordered to undress and presented with my prison uniform: a denim jacket, denim trousers, black shoes, and a blue-and-white-striped shirt. They also gave me a sheet and blankets.

I could not recognize the faces standing over me . . .

I was guided to my wing on the second floor. The warden's

keys rattled as he opened my cell door, and he smirked when he pushed me inside. I didn't have the energy to cuss at him. Pairs of eyes watched me through cell door vents and flaps.

The door clanged behind me and the sound seemed to filter through an echo chamber. Marley's "Burnin' and Lootin'" gatecrashed my mind again: *Oh God, I was a prisoner too!*

The smell of shit attacked my nostrils. My eyes watered. To my right was a bunk bed; the top was vacant. Below, I met the inquisitive gaze of a Rastafarian whose graying locks reached down to his waist. I guessed he was in his midforties. He had a lazy left eye, and a broad forehead. He had images of Black men and maps of Africa taped to the walls around his bed. I recognized Haile Selassie and Marcus Garvey. One portrait was of a Black Jesus Christ wearing an Egyptian ankh around his neck; another showed Shaka Zulu standing proud with his spear and long shield.

A small table and chair were placed beside a homemade bookshelf. A sink stood below a tiny wire-meshed window. On the other side of the cell was a curtain; the vile stench emitted from the other side of the screen. There, a slop bucket sat in a corner. If you wanted to do your business after seven p.m., you had to crouch over the bucket.

"What's your name, youthman?" the dread asked.

I didn't respond.

"We're going to be sharing the same space, so it'll be good if we can get along, you know. Ah unity me ah deal wid."

I ignored him.

"Sorry for the smell. Me cyan't tek the food here. It mash-up me belly. Me used to ital food. Babylon offerings are not good for I-man."

I climbed to my bunk and stretched out. I yawned a big yawn. I just wanted to sleep.

"You want someting to drink, youthman?"

I refused to engage with him. *Leave me the fuck alone.*

"Me overstand, youthman," he said. "Some people tek ah liccle time to mek the adjustment. Me name Simeon. But that's not what me mudder used to call me. Some call me the book master. Others call me the agitator."

I didn't utter a single word for the next three days. I even ignored fellow sufferahs who offered polite greetings. At mealtimes I stared into my plate as others spoke around me. I walked with my head down. I reverted to the silent episodes of my childhood when I refused to speak to social workers and staff.

I tried to create an image of my parents and imagine how they would react if they discovered that their son was serving time in prison.

In my cell, the smell didn't abate. Simeon suffered from stomach cramps and diarrhea.

On the fourth night, something exploded in my brain. I could not hold back my tortured soul any longer. My rage and bitterness, my sense of injustice. I had to release it.

I launched myself at Simeon, fists flailing. Unfortunately for me, he knew a little something about judo and karate. He made quick work of me and he gripped me in a hold.

My bawling began. I dredged up every bitter experience I had suffered. Tears gushed out of my eyes.

"Youthman! Youthman! What is wrong wid you?"

I eventually told my tale to the dread. He nodded slowly and took pity on me.

"Ah sufferah's tale fe true. Ah so it go. But don't let your past mash-up your future."

"Huh?"

"At least you have ah roof over your head and someting to eat tomorrow," Simeon reasoned. "Me cyan't keep it down but maybe you can. Ah whole heap ah young children all over the world don't have that luxury. So dry your tears, look up, and tek your stance again."

He related his own journey from the Jamaican parish of Westmoreland. With sadness, he spoke about his devout Christian family. His mother sang in the local church choir; his father grew crops. He was an only son.

In whispered conversations with a dreadlocked uncle who had come to visit, Simeon learned about the growing Rastafarian movement led by Leonard Howell. It fascinated him.

In 1951, at fourteen years of age, Simeon ran away from home to join a Rastafarian commune set up by Howell in Sligoville, St. Catherine, Jamaica. It was called Pinnacle because it was built on a hilltop. There, he learned the trade of a cabinet maker.

"Ah good place where me get me education. It opened me mind on many tings. Yes sah. You could see for miles and miles. Me also witnessed the living truth. We talked and reasoned long into the night."

It was a cooperative, where needs and services were traded with what skills you possessed. If Simeon wanted a new pair of pants, he'd build a chair for the seamstress. They lived off the land. Everyone was equal.

Jamaican police constantly raided the settlement. They demolished housing, beat up residents, smashed craftwork, and confiscated books and texts. They particularly wanted to destroy any copies of the *Kebra Nagast*—the Ethiopian bible.

Leonard Howell was arrested and charged with sedition. He served more than two years in prison. Simeon couldn't remember seeing him too often. "Him always inna jailhouse."

When Simeon wasn't subjected to police harassment, he performed his tasks during the day, helped tend the crops, smoked copious amounts of weed, and at night, around a small log fire, he was schooled by an Ethiopian Coptic priest named Reuben.

Simeon learned that when Moses led his people out of Egypt, it was because he had revived the cult of the singular god, Ra (the Egyptian word for *sun*). No other deities were to be worshipped. Moses adopted the faith of the so-called heretic pharoah, Akhenaten, who died in 1336 BC, a hundred or so years before Moses was born. He led slaves and workers of different races and nations who wanted to worship their one god out of Egypt. He strived to restore Akhenaten's rituals, ceremonies, and statues, and rebuild the city named after him.

The Coptic priest taught Simeon that the Knights Templar journeyed south into Africa as far as Ethiopia. They searched for the Ark of the Covenant and found many replicas and tabots in Ethiopian churches and temples. The artefacts and rituals they brought back with them to Europe inspired the birth of freemasonry.

One of the reasons why Mussolini's Italy wanted to invade Ethiopia centures later was to raze the churches to the ground to find the Ark, which was the Knights Templar's ultimate goal. Learning of their secret agenda, in 1307 Pope Clement V ordered their arrest and the seizure of their properties. He also wanted to take the Ark and anything else of religious value.

The Knights Templar, who had led the Crusades and fought for the Holy Land, were now hunted, tortured, and murdered all over Europe.

"Remember," the Coptic priest said to Simeon and his fellow students, "the pope wears the same headwear as

Akhenaten himself. The evidence is there. They are enacting the worship of Sun-Ra, the one-God."

"That's thousands of years ago, dread," I responded to Simeon. "How does that affect me now?"

"Study the images and iconography of the Virgin Mother with baby Jesus," Simeon said. "It's a blatant imitation of Isis, the Egyptian goddess, with her son, Horus. Remember, Alex, European men have always placed themselves in the narrative of world religions and history. For example, the Ten Commandments were lifted from the ancient Egyptian *Book of the Dead*. Jesus Christ and his family spent three years in Egypt. What did they learn there?"

"I don't know," I shrugged.

Simeon laughed. "They don't teach you that in Sunday school. They keep that part hidden. It's why they don't tell you about Prester John."

"Who's Prester John?"

"An African Christian king who ruled a nation in Asia before the Mongol empire conquered everybody in that part of the world. I'll tell you the story of Prester John just like Reuben tell it to me."

I found it difficult to absorb this new teaching. I struggled to comprehend it. The priest who presented sermons to the congregation at the Catholic church I went to in Shirley never sounded like this. My mind conjured images of Charlton Heston and Yul Brynner in *The Ten Commandments*.

"They have been lying to you," Simeon impressed on me. "Reset your mind. Rid yourself of the poison they have brainwashed you with. The Roman emperor Constantine did not include books and texts that told the story of Black people when he and his scribes edited the Bible. They erased our contribution, rewrote history. It was for the benefit of the white mon. We are not subservient or inferior to anyone!"

In 1954, the Jamaican military invaded the Pinnacle community, arresting everyone in sight. Simeon managed to escape and found a home in western Kingston with several of Leonard Howell's followers. Seeing their dreadlocks, locals branded them "blackheart men," and passed them on the other side of the street.

In an area of Kingston that was nicknamed "the dungle," Simeon worked as a carpenter and a cabinet maker. During evenings and weekends, he'd trek up the hills that overlooked Kingston where Rasta bredren held "grounations" and "reasonings." A Nyabinghi drummer offered a musical backdrop. They'd share a chalice and honor the coupling of King Solomon and the Queen of Sheba. They'd celebrate Haile Selassie's victory over Mussolini and mark his birthday. They hailed Marcus Garvey as a prophet and chanted down Babylon.

"You must read and educate yourself, Alex. If you don't know your past, you cyan't know your future. Know who you are and where you stand in the struggle."

The first book Simeon pressed into my hands was *The Black Jacobins* by C.L.R. James. "They will never teach this at school," he said. "No sah. The tale of Toussaint L'Ouverture and the Haitian Revolution and how he gave Napoleon ah bloody nose."

I couldn't even place Haiti on a map, but I accepted the book and read eagerly. It was incredible to learn that a slave army led by L'Ouverture beat the French and repelled the English and Spanish.

Other volumes I discovered on Simeon's bookshelf included *The Souls of Black Folk* by W.E.B. Du Bois, *Native Son* by Richard Wright, and *Invisible Man* by Ralph Ellison. The poetry of Langston Hughes. I gobbled up anything by Chester Himes and James Baldwin. Simeon introduced me to John Steinbeck's *The Grapes of Wrath*. "White sufferah's tale," he informed me.

He even recommended Margaret Mitchell's *Gone with the Wind*. "Yes, it racist," Simeon explained, "with false depictions of how Black people perceived their status as slaves. But you must learn how your oppressor thinks and how low they value ah Black life."

Reading Margaret Mitchell's text, I learned that there was very little thought or consideration from the author regarding Black people's hopes and aspirations. It failed to engage with how they interacted with their own families, how they reared their children, and what they tried to pass on to them. I raised this issue with Simeon.

"And nothing change," he said. "Until ah white society learns the same empathy and compassion for Black people as it has for themselves, racism will flourish."

"I don't know what you mean," I replied.

Simeon smiled in that way he had when he knew he had my attention. "When me hear Billie Holiday sing 'Strange Fruit,' where she's describing the lynching of Black people in the US, it brings tears to me eye. It nuh matter how many times me hear it."

"I've never heard of it," I said.

"When you leave this place, look for it. Listen to the lyrics. She paints an ugly picture. The point is, Alex, that until white people feel the same outrage and injustice as me feel when they hear that song, our lives will never be of the same value as dem. Me could say the same about Sam Cooke's 'A Change Is Gonna Come' or when Marvin Gaye sings 'What's Going On.' And the reggae songs that we sing together. You would think that to possess ah human heart, all white people would grow an empathy. But the truth is, too many of dem feel nothing. Dat's our fight."

"*Our* fight?"

"Yes, Alex, our eternal fight. It's why white policemen in England, the US, and South Africa can kill ah Black man in a prison cell and feel no shame, guilt, or remorse."

"They're just racist," I said.

"It's more than that, Alex. They are educated and *raised* to be racist and superior. Everyting around dem in their society tells dem they're better. It's how the British ruled nearly half the world."

PRISON SCHOOL

·······························

Four months into my sentence, Simeon handed me *The Auto-biography of Malcolm X.*

"Why are you giving me this?" I asked.

"Because you can relate to Malcolm X's journey," Simeon replied. "And learn from it."

"Learn what?"

Simeon grinned: he had my interest. "Malcolm X's papa was schooled by Marcus Garvey's words and movement. They looked to Mama Africa and Garvey wanted to build ah safe, prosperous place for Black people there. Malcolm lost his father when he was only six years old. He was placed in a foster home. He get himself messed up inna petty crime and they sent him to ah reform school. Ring any bells yet?"

"He was a Muslim, wasn't he? Not really interested in Muslims."

Simeon wagged a finger. "Don't be disrespectful, Alex. The book for me is not about his religion but about his journey. It's about ah man who refused to accept the circumstances of his birth. Do you overstand what me trying to teach you? *Refused.* He went on to achieve great tings and was one of the most powerful orators of the twentieth century."

"I don't think I could speak in public."

Simeon laughed from deep within his belly. "Don't you chat 'pon the mic?"

"That's different."

He leaned forward so I couldn't escape his intense gaze. "Alex, listen to me. Babylon not afraid of the angry Black mon. They've been dealing with him for hundreds of years. So when we get mad, when we lose our temper, they can say to everybody, *Look how the Black mon is wild. Look how him like ah savage. Look how they can't be trusted. We can't allow our women near dem!* What dem really afraid of is an educated Black mon. Yes, mon. Ah Black mon who knows him history, who knows his truth. Malcolm X knew his truth. They would have loved it if Malcolm X was inna crowd punching nuff white people. They could have dismissed everyting him ah say. You understand, Alex?"

"I think so."

"Remember, Alex," Simeon raised his voice, "every time you make ah breakthrough, every time you accomplish someting, everytime you create someting positive, every time you mek an achievement, that hurts the people who believe they're superior to you. It crumbles the walls of the people who hate you. Know that, Alex. Don't allow the circumstances of your birth to define you or dictate to you!"

"I'll try."

I made very few friends in prison. Simeon was the father I never had. There were days when I felt incredibly alone. At night, I tried to brace myself against it. I knew an attack would come. Depression was a constant shadow. Simeon encouraged me to sing; he reminded me of the power of the human voice.

"Sufferahs marched around the walls of Jericho for six

days singing their songs," he said with a glint in his eye; he loved his history. "And on the seventh time, they blew their trumpets and let out ah mighty chant. The walls came tumbling down. Yes sah, if you choose the right words, you can tear down the walls of any city or institution. Sing out, my youth!"

Dennis Brown was one of Simeon's favorite reggae artists as well. "Deliverance Will Come," from his *Words of Wisdom* album, has a place in my top three Dennis Brown songs. I can still hear Simeon's deep baritone as we sang it together: *For I have seen the land of my father in my visions, from the hills of captivity, plains . . .* It opens with blazing trumpets and a driving bass line, and its lyrics offer hope for a better tomorrow, more believable and relatable than any sermon I've heard from a preacher. The album cover itself is a true work of art. Check it out.

Message to my family here: When you host my funeral, play this and get everyone skanking. I'll be smiling.

Emancipation they say will never come . . .

"You're lost, Alex Wheatle," Simeon said to me one afternoon. "*Lost!*"

He secured a shirt over my eyes, twirled me around three times, and guided me to a corner of our cell. "Now, walk over to the other side."

I must have looked ridiculous when I reached out with my hands in my attempt to step to the far wall. It felt like I was reenacting Frankenstein's monster's first steps. Simeon's deep laugh embarrassed me.

Finally, he untied the shirt from my head. "That is your situation, Alex Wheatle. You don't know where you come from, and you don't know where you're going. Like ah lost sheep. Read up and educate yourself!"

I based my wise Jah Nelson character from *Brixton Rock* and *East of Acre Lane* on Simeon. How could I not? He was chuffed when he read both novels years later, and he only made one complaint: "You shoulda describe how me look like Harry Belafonte! Me mama say me favor him."

RELEASE

· ·

I was released from prison just before Christmas 1981.

On my last day, Simeon made me promise that I'd continue reading and educating myself about my people and my heritage.

"But I have no money to buy books, dread."

"Then forward to your library," Simeon urged. "Books are free in libraries. And the social services must have kept files on you, Alex Wheatle."

"You think so?"

"I know so. If there is one ting about the British, they love to make a record or file of everyting. Forward down to their offices and demand to see anyting written about you. They must have it."

"Okay."

"You must have a family out there," Simeon added. "Somewhere."

It was hard to imagine.

He gripped my shoulder. "Remember who you are, Alex Wheatle, and where you stand in the struggle. Your life is as valuable as any other. You and your ancestors have struggled through great tribulation. You're ah survivor. Never forget that."

* * *

Lambeth social services had kept my room vacant for me at Elm Park (they were unaware of my imprisonment for the first two months). I signed on again at the unemployment exchange and resumed my ritual of listening to reggae in Soferno B's shack and the General record store in the arcade. I checked out the flyers for the local reggae raves and blues parties.

It was good to breathe the Brixton air again. The traders' banter in the market invigorated me. The women looked prettier. The fruit appeared juicier. The sun shone brighter. I walked with a bounce in my step. Bionic, who sold live sound system cassette tapes in his tiny outlet, smiled as I strutted by.

I strolled up the Frontline and the badmen didn't look so intimidating, though I had no money to buy myself a draw of weed. I sat against the stained wall of a derelict property and observed the comings and goings, the joking, and the cursing.

DJs practiced their rhymes.

De bwoy bruk his tooth on Tumper's fried dumpling
Him run ah dentist to get plenty filling
Him kiss-up him gal and the filling drop out
Lord ah mercy, you shoulda hear the gal shout
She give the toothless bwoy one mighty big clout
And now the bwoy walk street wid ah donkey long-mout'

I was home.

Yes, mi friend, mi friend, me deh 'pon street again, Bob Marley and the Wailers sang in "Duppy Conqueror."

I needed some bass lines in my veins.

The mighty Sir Coxsone and the warrior Jah Shaka were

due to clash at Brixton Town Hall. They rarely played opposite each other in a dance. "Two big bull inna one pen."

I just had to be present.

I pulled on my mocassins and stepped down to what I considered my church.

By seven thirty p.m. the lobby was already jammed. Reggae-heads from all over London and beyond lined the wood-paneled walls of the assembly hall. One had carried inside a bongo drum. Women wore their red, gold, and green head wraps. Stepper boys (skankers), dressed in black tracksuits with red, gold, and green trims, waited impatiently onstage for the music to start. Jah Shaka taped his portrait of Haile Selassie behind his rig. Shaka bass-heads (myself included) watched the great man connect his valve amplifier, pre-amps, echo chamber, and siren box. Columns of eighteen-inch and mid-range bass speaker boxes were primed to deliver. Overhead, wires crisscrossed each other like noodles.

Festus, Coxsone's legendary selector, half spliff in mouth, watched from across the hall; Lloydie Coxsone towered behind him. Tension filled the air, blending with the sweet smell of collie weed.

Sir Coxsone tested their system first: "In tune to Sir Coxsone Outernational, the A-one greatest sound inna the world."

I had never heard Coxsone play better. "Homeward Bound" by Creation Stepper got the skankers onstage knee-bopping and contorting like they had never stepped before. "Good Old Days" by Ras Midas had the crowd in a frenzy.

Jah Shaka looked on impassively. Eventually he reached for his dub plate box. The black wax spun on the turntable, no record label stamped on it. The crowd held its breath. The stepper boys took a break. Then the horn section kicked in. And the percussion: "The Gates of Zion." Michael Prophet's mournful lead vocal rode over a ferocious bass line. *Ethiopia is where I wanna be.* It was produced by Yabby You and mixed by Scientist at King Tubby's quarter tower.

Reggae-heads erupted. Some might have even combusted. Everyone in the dance skanked for dear life and joy. It felt almost like an exorcism in reverse. The spirit hit you. Shaka the great warrior. When he played the instrumental version, he employed the full range of his siren box. The crowd was delirious.

I have never seen such freedom of expression and lack of inhibition before or since.

SEEDS OF MY CREATIVITY

....

There was the inevitable low following the Brixton Town Hall session. I had to combat loneliness at Christmas yet again. I didn't want to wander around the Brixton streets feeling dejected. I tried to ignore the Christmas advertisements on television. Bitter memories of my childhood resurfaced. *You're better off than so many children inna the world, Alex Wheatle,* I remembered Simeon telling me. *Tek your stance again and lift up your head! When depression licks, you must vent it out, mon. Nuh let it linger inna your head. Express it! Words are power.*

I bought a small notepad and two black Biros from a corner store in Elm Park. I also purchased a single cigarette so I could wrap two big heads: one for Christmas Eve and the other for Christmas Day.

Christmas Eve night, I settled on my bed and pressed play on my Dennis Brown cassette. *What about the half that's never been told . . .*

I lit my spliff and meditated.

I exhaled through my nose.

Words came to me:

3 A Better Place
Self-esteem
Belief

Dear Nobody,

I hear your wailing every night. My heart senses your pain. My brain stores your memories. I have lived through your agonies. My old friend Loneliness never leaves me alone. The triplets Brutality, Contempt, and Insignificance visit you too often. Trust has long ago abandoned you. She has gone to the place where Roots now resides. Hug has never shown her face. Love has never introduced herself. Unworthiness wants to take you out for the day. Low esteem always wants to party. Empty birthdays of the past fill you. Christmas has always mocked you. Your brother Rage now sleeps with you. But I'm coming back, Nobody. So hold on to Hope. I know he's tiny and fragile. I know he's sick. I know you cannot see him in the dark— you have to concentrate hard to hear his voice. But he is there. Nurture him, nurse him. One day he might grow big.

Yes, I'm coming back for you, Nobody. It's been a long road full of wrong signs and deep holes—the odd mountain too. And I have been blind and one-eyed for so long. For many years I didn't want to accept you. I tried to deny you. But you lived in my head. I don't know how you got in. But you did. Yes, you did, you and Hope. Most of the time you were both asleep, recovering from the wounds Trauma inflicted upon you. But then you both woke. I pretended I didn't hear you. I tried to wish you away. I broke down when you and Hope were both screaming at me. I was exhausted,

spent. You and Hope too. But I remember your words
before the fall:

> *Motherless children,*
> *If no one loves you in this world,*
> *Make a start and love yourself.*

> *Yes, I'm coming for you, Nobody. And when I finally*
> *bless my eyes on you, I'll rename you. Yes, you're going to*
> *be Somebody.*

> *Yours sincerely,*
> *Your older self*

I had no idea that the above piece would be published
thirty-eight years later in *Common People: An Anthology of*
Working-Class Writers, edited by a very good friend of mine,
Kit de Waal.

If there are any aspiring writers reading this reggae-ography,
my advice to you is to never throw anything away.

BLIND DATE

. . . .

My bredren Floyd, who had the keys to his mum's white Datsun on weekends, informed me that he had been invited to a family friend's celebration in Battersea. To raise my spirits, he asked me to come along and "live in the land of the living" instead of feeling sorry for myself in Elm Park. He also told me that the man of the house who hosted the gathering had a pretty daughter. "She's well ripe," Floyd said. He dated one of her friends. "But don't go on like a Brixton hound sniffing a bitch inna Brockwell Park. Come proper! She's an A-class girl."

"I'm not sure about this," I replied.

"Wheats!" Floyd raised his voice. "Step to your bathroom and fling 'way your BO. Slap on some deodorant and pull on some decent garms. Fix up your head. Me nuh want you looking like a ghetto cruff. So come slick and ready. Me sick and tired of you looking so damn miserable. Carry on your ways and you will turn into an extra blanket for your damn bed. Get your fockin' backside inna gear."

I climbed into the backseat of the Datsun. Errol, Floyd's cousin, occupied the front passenger seat. Dennis Brown pumped out of the car stereo. We hit Acre Lane and drove along the south side of Clapham Common.

Floyd wasn't wrong: Beverley was very attractive, and then some.

"Wheats," Floyd barked at me, "stop looking 'pon the nice girl and step forward and chat to her."

I just couldn't summon the courage to approach her. I stared into my rum and Coke. Maybe my prison term had further eroded my confidence.

On the drive back to Brixton, Errol and Floyd wouldn't let it go. "Can't believe it," Floyd complained. "Man let me down! Take the man to dance, introduce him to a nice girl, and him stand up and say nutten! Wheats, no more setups for you! You may as well have stayed in prison and fucked the holes in the walls!"

Before he dropped me off at my hostel, he wrote down Beverley's phone number. "If you ever find your balls, call her!"

Four days later, I made the call. Her father picked up. I dropped the phone like it was a hot spare rib in my fingers.

I think it was on the third attempt that I managed to get Beverley on the line. I stuttered an introduction: "I . . . I was the guy with Floyd and Errol."

"Yes," she said, "me remember. The quiet one! You remember you have ah tongue?"

Somehow, I managed to arrange a date. It was a Sir Lloyd blues dance in Brixton. She took the 37 bus from Battersea Rise and I met her at the stop outside Brixton Town Hall. She wore a burgundy camel coat, and her hair was hot-combed into a trendy wavy style.

As I stepped inside with her, I felt like I had won the jackpot. Her reggae-head status was an added bonus. We rocked to Carroll Thompson, Sister Love, Alpha, and many more lovers' rock artists.

I paid for Beverley's cab home and trod back to Elm Park saying to myself, *Wheats, don't fuck it up!*

Beverley studied art at Brixton College, but she had other responsibilities too. Her mother had passed away when she was only nine years old. She was the oldest of five siblings and had taken on many of her mother's duties.

We dated intermittently over the following months, attending family gatherings, parties, blues dances, boat cruises, movies, and simply hanging out playing reggae music. I'd often turn up at her home on a Friday evening with food from Kentucky Fried Chicken or McDonald's. I got to know her father Franklin and her siblings. One night, Franklin insisted on taking me out to a pub where he interrogated me about my intentions toward his daughter. Beverley and I committed to each other in the latter half of 1982.

I had something to live for, a life to share. Loneliness knew I had a shield and defender—he now attacked me only once or twice a month instead of every other day.

Bev and I finally got married in 1998, and the song that we took the floor to was "In Loving You" by Junior English, a gentle lovers' rock ballad with a horn intro that seduces you into the slow dance. Many Jamaican singers were heavily influenced by Curtis Mayfield's songbook and falsetto vocals. "In Loving You," a version of a Mayfield track titled "Love to Keep You in My Mind," was a classic of that era.

TRACING MY ROOTS

....

During the weeks that led to my release from Wormwood Scrubs, at night Simeon repeated a mantra that he didn't want me to forget. He quoted Marcus Garvey: *A people without the knowledge of their past history, origin, and culture is like a tree without roots.*

I reflected on those words on New Year's Eve, 1981.

On January 3, 1982, my nineteenth birthday, I made a decision: I wanted to trace my family.

A few days later, I marched down to the social services area three office on Herne Hill Road. When I met the duty social worker, I demanded to read my files.

"You have to make an appointment," he said.

"Why do I have to make an appointment? The files are about *me*. They should belong to me. Who else is gonna be interested in reading them?"

"All files of children who spent time in care are legally owned by Lambeth Council."

I gave the man a fierce side-eye. "This is fucking ridiculous."

"I don't make the rules."

I made an appointment for the following week.

* * *

This is what I looked like in 1982

The day before my next meeting at the social services office, I was sick with nerves. *What if I discover that both of my parents are dead? What if I find out that my mother gave me up cos I was too ugly? What if my so-called mum and dad gave false names to the social services? What if? What if? What if?*

My brain fizzed with a multitude of bad scenarios.

I tried to relax by playing a Bob Marley cassette: *Could you be loved and be loved? Don't let them fool ya . . .*

I considered postponing the appointment.

I can't do this. But do I want to live my life without knowing who I'm related to? How many more Christmases will I have to suffer through? How many more awkward conversations will I have to endure when a young lady is interested in me and she asks me about my family? You're a somebody, Alex. Simeon thinks so. I have discovered my cultural identity, now I need to find my family bloodline.

I made my way down to Herne Hill Road and paused at the entrance, sucking in a long breath. *Your life might change from this very moment. Could you be loved? Can you handle rejection?*

Waiting in the lobby was a stressed mother with her two young boys. One of them played with a matchbox car, rolling it into the walls and laughing as he did so. "Stop it! Stop it! Stop it!" the mum screamed, then broke down in tears.

I asked if she was okay.

A social worker emerged and led her and her two sons to a room.

As I waited impatiently for the duty social worker to bring my files, I wondered what story lay behind the distressed young woman with her two kids.

Twenty minutes following the time of my appointment, the duty social worker finally appeared. He wore corduroy trousers and a checked jacket with leather elbow patches. His long hair didn't have any acquaintance with a comb.

"Follow me," he said.

He led me down a flight of stairs to the basement where there were storage cupboards, cardboard boxes, a small kitchen, and a couple of side rooms.

I found myself in a space that had a small round table and two wooden chairs set opposite each other. Resting on the table was a thick file bound with elastic bands. My full name was written in thick black felt tip on the cover: *Alec Alphonso Wheatle.*

For some reason, I didn't want to share the intimacy of

my young life with a stranger. I snatched the file and made a run for it out of the room, up the stairs, and out of the building. I didn't stop running until I reached Ruskin Park. I found a bench, opened the file, and read the first page:

London Borough of Lambeth
CHILDREN'S DEPARTMENT
Assumption of parental rights
Alec Alphonso Wheatle (03/01/1963)

Alphonso, an illegitimate child, was received into care under Section 1, Children Act 1948, on 17.4.64, as the private foster mother with whom he was placed by his putative father was unable to continue caring for him. His mother, a married woman, entrusted Alphonso to him. She has returned to Jamaica.

He was placed in a Council nursery initially and transferred in February 1966 to the children's home where he is now living. On admission, he was suffering from severe eczema, but this has improved, and he is making good progress.

His putative father, who voluntarily contributed to his maintenance for a short period, has had no contact with him since October 1964. When he was interviewed in November 1965, he refused to make further contributions . . .

It is recommended that parental rights and powers in respect of Alphonso W. be assumed in accordance with Section 2 of the Children Act 1948, as extended by Section 48 (1) of the Children and Young Persons Act 1963 . . .

Tears dripped down my cheeks as I continued reading.

Something reached deep inside me and twisted the core of my being.

I hated the very thought of my father.

I'm still baffled as to why they referred to me as *Alphonso*, which is my middle name.

Here's an entry from Ladywell Residential Nursery, dated August 17, 1965:

London Borough of Lewisham
CHILDREN'S DEPARTMENT
LADYWELL RESIDENTIAL NURSERY
Slagrove Place, Ladywell Road, SE13

August 17, 1965

Edw. R. Murphy, D.F.C. M.A.
Children's Officer
London Borough of Lambeth
45c, Streatham Hill SW2

Dear Mr. Murphy,
Re—Alphonso WHEATLE (3.1.63)
Admitted here 7.4.64
Thank you for your letter concerning this child who suffers from severe eczema.
Since he has been with us, he has been three times an inpatient at Sydenham's Children's Hospital and is still attending outpatients.
I am afraid that his prognosis regarding his skin condition is poor and he is likely to require treatment for many years yet.
He needs daily and continuous cleansing and appli-

*cations of ointments and I would suggest a residential
school with sick bay and trained nurse facilities as a suitable placement.*

*I am anxious he should be transferred from Ladywell
Nursery since we often have to vaccinate young children
against smallpox, and on each occasion Alphonso is at special risk and has yet to be kept in isolation . . .*

*Yours sincerely
T.V. Mendelsohn*

It was quite traumatizing to discover the reality of my
early life. I had to take breaks from reading the documents
but I continued studying the file until nightfall. I can't remember eating anything that day or, indeed, the day after.

Here's an excerpt of a social worker's report from a visit
on September 4, 1969:

*. . . Alphonso appears to be making satisfactory progress in
the cottage. Loves swimming (can swim 4 strokes), football, and cricket and participates with the other boys in
these activities. Appears to be coming more confident. Still
has bad bouts of asthma (eczema—recently had temp. of
102 degrees and is on course of penicillin).*

*Miss Joyce Cook (housemother) tells me she has been
most concerned over his progress at school. Educationally
his progress is good, and he appears of at least average intelligence. However, she has received various complaints
from his form teacher of his aggressiveness and violent
behaviour toward other children. She has reason to believe that he is frequently sent out of the classroom for long
periods and physically punished. She feels that Alphonso is*

*a deprived boy needing an understanding approach and
a lot of individual attention and is very anxious of the
effect of this rather punitive approach by form teacher. She
has in fact spoken to Mr. Holman (Shirley Oaks superintendent) about this and he shares her concern. He is said
to be investigating the possibility of Alphonso attending an
outside school (for delicate children?) and Mrs. Winch saw
Alphonso recently for this purpose. Her report is in the file.*

*. . . Saw Alphonso and watched him playing football
with two other boys. He naturally was showing off but
displayed his talent.*

*I shared Miss Cook's concern over the effect of a re-
pressive approach at school on a boy needing such a high
degree of individual attention. It seems likely to encour-
age his aggressiveness . . .*

C.A. Jarrold
Child Care Officer

When I read this document, I didn't know whether to
laugh or cry. I apologize to the children who I was aggressive
to. At least I had discovered the circumstances that led me to
attend St. Giles School.

Miss Joyce Cook should have been concerned over her own
repressive approach. She was my chief guardian but was responsible for my constant state of terror for most of my childhood.

Society needs to ask questions and learn why a six-year-
old boy would act so aggressively and display such violent
behavior.

Here is another entry by Ms. C.A. Jarrold dated January
15, 1970:

Alphonso feeling very sorry for himself as he had just developed chicken-pox on top of a bout of eczema. Loss of appetite and very lethargic. Miss Cook enquired whether we had any news of Alphonso's proposed transfer to outside school for delicate children. She recently had an encouraging report from Alphonso's new form teacher re: improved conduct and performance at school. Nevertheless, she still feels Alphonso would greatly benefit from the transfer, as the school proposed has a very good reputation. They feel Alphonso is an intelligent boy whose progress and performance will suffer from absences, unless in more specialised school environment. Said I was still waiting news from Croydon Education Department.

Also discussed Alphonso's need for a regular "aunt" and "uncle" contact—he tends now to develop psychosomatic symptoms on visiting days if other children have visitors.

On June 11, 1970, Ms. C.A. Jarrold recorded another visit:

Alphonso is looking forward to commencing to his new school (St. Giles School for delicate children).

Student and I took Alphonso out for the afternoon for a drive into the country. He opened out considerably and was quite a responsive little boy. Very interested and observant in what we passed. Fascinated by farms and he counted 14 en route.

We had tea in Westerham which Alphonso thoroughly enjoyed. He was not self-conscious in the restaurant.

All I can add is, thank you very much, Ms. C.A. Jarrold. If only I'd had the courage to inform you what was really occurring inside Holly House. If only.

Here's another social worker entry dated February 14, 1974:

Concern of teaching staff over choice of schools for Alphonso. Alphonso does not seem to be happy with Mark's choice.

(Years later, Mark, real name William Hook, a swimming instructor who worked and lived in our cottage, was convicted of sexually abusing many children at four South London children's home institutions. He was sentenced by Judge Kenneth MacCray for ten years at Kingston Crown Court. In his closing remarks the judge said: "This is a sordid tale of depravity, self-gratification, and corruption ... you robbed children of their innocence by embarking upon classic grooming techniques.")

"Mark" wanted to decide which secondary school I attended.

1/ St. Joseph's (Catholic)
2/ Ingram
3/ Bishop Thomas Grant
4/ Hayling Manor

The staff feel that the transition from primary to secondary will be traumatic for Alphonso.

I rang St. Joseph's who did not give out much hope of Alphonso being accepted there due to his lack of knowledge of Catholicism.

Alphonso attended the interview with Mark, who was hoping to arrange for Alphonso to visit a priest in order to learn about Catholicism. I feel this is a very unwise suggestion ... There is little chance of Alphonso being accepted at St. Joseph's, it is completely unnecessary.

The teacher, Mrs. Bradley, and headmaster Mr. Foster

at Alphonso's school are concerned about his reluctance to talk about his life at Holly House. They find difficulty in communicating with Miss Cook at times and feel this uncertainty at school is based largely on his instability at the home. He became extremely upset after very small incidents which perhaps have led to a cross word by a member of staff.

They are all of the opinion that the other choices for Alphonso are extremely unsuitable both because of their location and because none of Alphonso's friends will be going to these schools.

Mrs. Bradley would like to take part in a discussion with Miss Cook and myself about Alphonso, particularly to try and reach some agreement regarding his secondary education.

I spoke to Alphonso who is quite keen to attend Shirley High School rather than the schools Mark suggested. I reassured him that my presence at the school was not to discuss his behaviour and that I had received a very good report on him—this pleased him immensely.

Mr. Hedman (a foster carer) has visited him once at Holly House and is keen to take Alphonso home for weekends. He feels Alphonso will be happy to accept his offer.

Mr. Hedman has a friend interested in fostering a child such as Alphonso. His name is Mr. Smith and he has West Indian heritage. I am arranging a meeting with him in the near future. Obviously, any movement toward Alphonso going to stay with him (even for short periods) would have to be introduced very slowly . . . Alphonso's reactions and feelings would have to be carefully monitored.

Ms. P.A. Eastwood

There are enough red flags to put a halt to numerous grand prix in the above document. Reading this sent a chill curling around my spine.

Joyce Cook handed me a brutal beating with a rolling pin because I refused to go to St. Joseph's School. I stopped attending Catholic church and suffered another hiding. Yet William Hook wanted to send me to St. Joseph's Catholic school in Norwood and was quite explicit about me meeting a priest to teach me Catholicism.

You must wonder why.

I believe I escaped a fresh hell awaiting me.

Let me place it on record that William Hook never sexually abused me. However, he did often remark that my eczema was ugly. He smoked Dunhill cigarillos, and at times he offered me enough pennies for me to buy a comic if I jogged up to Fred Dawes's newsagents to buy him a packet.

The relationship between Mr. Hedman and me wasn't allowed to develop, and I never met his West Indian friend who had expressed a desire to foster a child.

Again, we must ask why.

I remember that my social worker at the time, Ms. P.A. Eastwood, moved on to another position shortly after she filed the above report. This was particularly difficult to cope with: you learn to trust an adult, and then they're gone, never to be seen again.

I don't think I ever trusted another social worker again following Ms. Eastwood's departure.

Fuck 'em.

I brought my file home and read throughout the night.

The big reveal for me was when I discovered I had five siblings—four sisters and one brother.

It was difficult to comprehend that I shared my mother's blood with five other human beings. I tried to imagine what they looked like and if they enjoyed the same things I did. Did they sing along to the Jackson 5 and the Supremes? Could they dance like the Temptations and the Four Tops? Could they perform the "Car Wash" line dance? How did they celebrate Christmas and birthdays? What were their grades like at school? What sports were they interested in? Were any of them reggae-heads? That would have been a bonus.

Just knowing that somewhere out there in the wide world I had family gave me an incredible boost of confidence.

I'm *not* a nobody. I'm a somebody. I *can* be loved.

PART III

IF YUH HAVE A PAPER, YUH MUST HAVE A PEN

MY OWN HOME

....

In the spring of 1982, Lambeth Council offered me a council flat on Glanville Road, near Brixton Hill. Because their social services department had a duty to care for me up to eighteen years of age, the council was obliged to house me when I departed Elm Park too. From my bedroom window, I could see the unused windmill that dominated the landscape in this corner of Brixton.

I bought a secondhand cooker and fridge from a nearby store, asked my friend Floyd to help transport my belongings, and I whitewashed the walls with paint given to me by a former colleague who worked for Lambeth Council.

For the first few weeks, I slept on a mattress on the floor. I didn't have much, but it was my first home all my own.

I rarely cooked for myself. If I did, I ate corned beef or pilchards with Uncle Ben's rice or instant mashed potatoes. Tin cans of sausage and beans were also a staple. There was a fish-and-chip shop nearby, and I bought my favorite chicken patty and chips almost every day. Breakfast was often a packet of custard creams. Lunch was a dry bread roll. I always tried to save a little extra so I could purchase at least one 7" record from Soferno B's or the General record store.

In the dancehalls, King Yellowman was one of the most

popular DJs emerging from Jamaica. I was fascinated to discover that he was raised in the Alpha Boys children's home in Kingston, Jamaica. It was administered by nuns—the Sisters of Mercy. I was proud to learn that many of Jamaica's most celebrated musicians spent much of their childhoods in the facility, including Don Drummond, Rico Rodriguez, Johnny "Dizzy" Moore, Leroy Smart, Tommy McCook, and Cedric Brooks.

I still worked for cash on building sites until I was hired by a company nearby on Lyham Road that imported cane and bamboo furniture. My task was to repair any item that had been damaged in transit from overseas. I enjoyed my job, especially as I was permitted to bring in a small boom box to accompany me in the warehouse.

Much of my downtime I spent on my own. If I could afford it, I bought more reggae albums. Anything by Dennis Brown, Gregory Isaacs, Sugar Minott, Linval Thompson, Barrington Levy, and of course King Yellowman, I added to my collection. The one I meditated to most was *Right Time* by the Mighty Diamonds. I kept going back to the track "I Need a Roof." I felt not so alone anymore when I heard the beautiful harmonies: *I need a roof over my head, and bread on my table . . .*

As I write these words, I still feel incredibly saddened by the murder of Tabby Diamond, lead singer of the Mighty Diamonds, in April 2022. His songs will outlive me and my children's children. A few days later, his fellow bandmate Bunny Diamond also passed away. I hope they knew of the comfort and upliftment their songs offer to sufferahs like myself.

I wondered what kind of home my siblings were raised in and where they attended school or clocked on for work. *Do any of them resemble me in any way?* It would freak me out if I discovered a brother who looked like me.

For my whole life I'd had company—even in prison. Living by myself in my new abode, loneliness attacked me once again, but reggae music provided a shield for me, as did the books I read. At the Brixton library, I discovered Claude McKay, Zora Neale Hurston, Maya Angelou, and many others.

I purchased a new notebook and began to fill it with my thoughts, my memories, my rage, and my life experiences. I wrote poetry as well as DJ and song lyrics. Little did I know then that this journal would provide the foundation for my first two novels, *Brixton Rock* and *East of Acre Lane*. They would be published years later, in 1999 and 2000.

I sang my words softly at night, almost as if praying before I retired to bed. "Singing is good for the soul," Simeon always encouraged me.

You can see how heavily influenced I was by Dennis Brown's "Deliverance Will Come" and the teachings of Simeon:

Fear not, my bredren, for we shall gather the sweet fruits of our fathers' toils
And the wails of our mothers shall transform into joyous smiles of emancipation
Brood not, for the pain of our heavy heart shall beat in the oppressor's chest
Weep not, for our sore wounds shall heal, and only the scars shall remain of our mighty struggles
Concentrate your ears, for the hymn of our motherland is now heard among us
Be of sure foot, for we shall be led to the blessed Greenland by the righteous songwriters who play the golden harps of deliverance

*Their footprints shall be employed by the gifted musicians
and the spirit dancers
Unchain your doubts, for our sufferation shall be no more
Sing out loud, for glorious things have been written of our
triumphant redemption
Yield not, for the oppressor shall not find haven from the
tables of judgement
Stride proudly, for our path has been signposted by the
martyrs of equal rights
The end of our perilous journey is near, and I can see the
ark of our homeland glitter in the distance
Fear not, my bredren, for we shall soon be free*

Spring and summer 1982 was a very creative, productive time
for me. Some pieces, like the above, I never performed on my
sound system; others I chanted in public for Crucial Rocker.

I had a bredren who lived on the sixteenth floor of a tower
block near Herne Hill that overlooked Brockwell Park. Even
on a sweltering day, he refused to open his windows in case a
bird might fly in.

I came out with a lyric:

*Me seh life inna Brixton nah easy
Me seh life inna Brixton nah easy
Me daddy cyan't afford de money fe me tea
Me mudder cyan't afford de electricity
De council nah fix de roof above we
De bird dem ah fly in and shit 'pon me
Me daddy sick and tired of redundancy
We had to sell our new color TV
De rat dem ah come in and have ah party
Me look out me window and see ah plane next to me*

Me feel de flat sway when we catch de strong breeze
We are so high we cyan't see de trees
De flat is so damp dat me brudder start wheeze
De shitstem is bringing us down to our knees
But de politician dem nah listen to we pleas
Me seh life inna Brixton nah easy
Me seh life inna Brixton nah easy
Me don't know why we left from de Caribbean Sea . . .

The above lyrics found their way into my fiction years later.

I felt I had finally found a purpose in life.

Simeon had been released from prison and I visited him in his Kennington flat. He didn't own a TV. There were books everywhere, even in his bathroom. Piled up on a cabinet beside his bed were letters from abroad: Jamaica. I asked who they were from.

"Just family," he replied. "No big ting."

From his expression, I knew it *was* a big deal, though I didn't press him on it.

"You say you have written ah liccle something?" he asked.

I was eager to perform my songs and lyrics for him. When I concluded, he nodded and smiled. "You find your talent," he said. "Yes, mon. Me have to call you Naphtali from now on."

"What's that?"

"You're January born, right?"

"Yes, the third of January," I said.

"You're one of the Twelve Tribes of Israel," Simeon explained. "Naphtali means to *struggle*, or I prefer the *sufferah*. That's where your words come from, out of sufferation. To speak the sufferah's truth is your gift. Share the sufferah's tale.

Use your gift wisely or the Most High will tek it away. Ah so it go."

"I'll try," I said.

"Don't abuse it . . . use it."

LEARNING RESPONSIBILITY

Beverley gave birth to our first son, Marvin, in May 1983. As I held the new baby in my arms, a sudden fear wrapped around me: *Can I be responsible for this life? Can I really take on the duties of a father? Am I capable?*

Initially, I shied away from that burden. It was difficult to wrench myself away from the lifestyle I had developed in Brixton: following favorite sound systems all over London and beyond, smoking herb and playing dominoes with friends until the early hours, and bluesing and partying every weekend. Plus there was my inability to restrain my temper and remain in a secure job.

When Marvin was about six months old, I gave up my place and we moved into a council flat on Nine Elms Lane, near the Battersea Dogs & Cats Home. That location wasn't as developed as it is now with new buildings and plush estates lining the entire length of the road; the American embassy was recently relocated there.

Every Sunday morning I'd take Marvin for a walk in Battersea Park, no matter the weather, to give Beverley a break. As Marvin crawled on the grass or slept in my arms, I vowed that I *had* to be in his life. He would never be lonely.

I wondered if my own parents shared the same instincts

for protecting and nurturing their children. Surely, despite my father giving me up to social services, he and my mother must have felt some natural affinity and connection with me.

I learned while raising Marvin and my two other children, Tyrone and Serena, who were born in 1984 and 1985, that a young child can offer pure, unconditional love, not yet spoiled by the teen years or the baggage that may arrive later. I felt so proud that they looked up at me as a source of love. They smiled and laughed at me whenever I arrived home from work or anywhere else. They wrapped their little arms around my neck. They cared not that I'd had a traumatic start to life and didn't possess any reference points or role models in becoming a father. They loved me anyway. I was their dad.

There were also challenges along the way, including periods of unemployment, the return of my self-worth and loneliness demons, and difficulties forming relationships with Beverley's extended family and attempting to explain my own background to them.

"Not even a cousin?" one asked.

I shook my head and hoped I wouldn't be interrogated further.

Some might consider it trivial, but I used to get terrified that I had somehow messed up the milk formula. I had to learn not to be triggered when the kids cried. To this day, I find it difficult to hear a baby's wailing.

This all compelled me to consider trying to track down my own parents and the rest of my family. *Where do I start? Maybe the telephone book?*

As I began tracing my roots, I shelved my creative writing, only returning to it if Beverley was away visiting her family.

Brown Sugar's version of Curtis Mayfield's "I'm So Proud"

will always be one of my favorite lovers' rock tracks. Pauline, Caron, and Kofi could all sing lead vocals, and they recorded some of the most unforgettable lovers' rock tracks in history, including "I'm in Love with a Dreadlocks" and "Black Pride."

Many years later, I was fortunate enough to meet Pauline Catlin-Reid, one of the founding members of Brown Sugar. Beverley and I watched her perform songs from a new album at the Ritzy in Brixton. I was then honored to write the liner notes for one of her later albums: *Catch the Boat* was released in 2018, with Pauline now recording under the name Shezekiel.

Sometimes you do get to meet your musical heroes.

DIGGING UP THE PAST

The crown prince of reggae, Dennis Brown, was born on February 1, 1957. He was a child protégé. It was difficult to believe he was only six years older than me. At thirteen years of age, he walked into Coxsone Dodd's recording studio at 13 Brentford Road, Kingston 5, Jamaica, and recorded the *No Man Is an Island* album for release on the Studio One label in 1970.

The maturity and control of the lead vocals are astonishing for someone so tender in years. He sounded like a seasoned professional. I reflected on the title track as I considered tracing my family. *You can't live in this world all by yourself* . . .

As I raised my young children, the specter of my parents continually nagged a corner of my mind. Beverley warned me that it could result in devastation if they rejected me again or failed to acknowledge me.

Recorded in my social services files were the last known addresses of my parents. My father had lived at 13 Northlands Street, off Coldharbour Lane between Brixton and Camberwell. I made a house call.

The white owner informed me that they had never heard of an Alfred Wheatle, but that I should inquire at another home on the street where the family had lived for over twenty years.

Anticipation grew in me as I walked toward the terraced residence. When a West Indian man opened the door, hope swelled in my heart. He narrowed his eyes as he checked me from scalp to toe. *Maybe I should've put on a nice pair of slacks, a shirt, and a tie.*

"Good evening," I said. "Do you know of an Alfred Wheatle who lived at number 13 in the mid-1960s?"

The man thought about it and rubbed his chin, then closed the front door behind him. "Ah Jamaican mon used to own dat house," he said. "And he rented out rooms to single West Indians. It wasn't too easy finding ah place back then. When me first come in the '50s it was an Irish woman who rented out ah place for me just around the corner. English people did not want to tek us in."

"Did you know Mr. Wheatle?" I asked again.

"What do him look like?"

"Like me, I suppose. He's my dad."

The man scratched his eyebrow. "You sure?"

"Yes, I'm sure. I can show you my birth certificate."

"That is not necessary."

"Did you know him?" I pressed.

"It was ah long time ago," the man said. "People come and go. There was ah somebody . . . him was taller than you. Ah carpenter—"

"That's him!" I interrupted. "My dad was a carpenter! That's what it says on my birth certificate."

"Me sure me did bump into him at ah party or someting. But me never know him too good."

"Do you know of anyone who might have been a close friend?" I asked.

"People move on, you know. Get married, move outta the area, decide to move abroad."

"Nobody?"

"Sorry me cyan't help you. Me wish you luck. Have ah good evening." He turned and opened his front door and disappeared.

I closed my eyes and stood still for a few seconds, realizing that my quest would be much more difficult than I had imagined.

I traveled to Chapter Road, Neasden, in North London, the last known address of my mother. Her birth name was Almira Panceta DaCosta. On seeing me, one white resident slammed the door in my face, perhaps believing I was scouting his place for a potential burglary, or maybe he suspected I was a Jehovah's Witness. It was demoralizing.

I settled on my original idea of finding an address under a Wheatle name in the phone book. I was fortunate that the Wheatle listings were not as lengthy as the Smiths or the Browns.

My first call was to Appach Road, Brixton, only a ten-minute trod from my former address in Elm Park. According to the phone book, a Mr. H. Wheatle lived there.

When I arrived, there was a Cortina Mark IV parked out front. I thumbed the doorbell, closed my eyes for a short second, and waited for someone to answer. A moment later, a young Black woman opened the door. She looked about the same age as me, maybe a year or two older. As she stared at me, I struggled to utter a greeting.

"I'm ... I'm Alex Wheatle. Is this ... is this the house of Mr. Wheatle?"

"Yes," she said, "he's my dad. And you're definitely a Wheatle."

"How ... how ... ?"

"Your complexion," she explained. "And your forehead. Broad like a Wheatle!"

My heart sang. I smiled. *At last! At last! I've found family! Maybe Mr. Wheatle is an uncle. Perhaps this young woman is my cousin.*

"Come in," she said. "My name is Sharon. Sharon Wheatle. My dad's name is Hubert."

Sharon led me down a hallway and into the kitchen. I didn't have to be told who Hubert was. He sat at the kitchen table eating his dinner. We shared the same shade of skin complexion, forehead, and dark eyes.

"My God," he said, "ah Wheatle for true!"

"Do . . . do you know my dad?" I asked excitedly. "Alfred, Alfred's his name. He's tall. A carpenter."

Hubert slowly chewed a piece of chicken. "Me don't have any brudder or uncle who name Alfred," he finally said. "But me grandfader had plenty brothers that me don't know about."

"So, we could be related?"

"Yes, of course," Hubert said. "The Wheatle family originate from Manchester in Jamaica. Come meet the rest of the family."

Hubert introduced me to his wife, Sylvia. She offered me dinner and I happily accepted. As I ate my meal, I met Hubert's two sons, Tony and Stuart, and his youngest daughter, Christine. Jean, Hubert and Sylvia's oldest daughter, wasn't home.

Everyone accepted me warmly and didn't doubt my claim of being a Wheatle for a millisecond. It was an added bonus that they all loved reggae. Tony was actually a member of the Studio One sound system based in Brixton—it was a coincidence that I had attended one of their ram-jam dances.

Before I departed, Hubert promised me that he'd call his

cousin Persia, who knew more than most about the Wheatle family tree and where they had spread to. Apparently, there were Wheatles in Catford, Tottenham, Toronto, the USA, and "ah whole heap in Jamaica."

I went home that night feeling I *belonged.*

I'm somebody.

A week or so later, I met Persia in her flat in Tulse Hill. She, too, commented on my forehead and complexion. "You're definitely a Wheatle," she said.

She couldn't quite place my father Alfred in the family tree, but she mentioned that some branches and twigs were unaccounted for. "My grandfader had many brothers," she told me. "They were born over eighty, maybe ninety years ago, and they made their own way into the world. Maybe your grandfader is one of dem. Nuh worry, Alex, we will find that twig."

Persia put me in touch with an Aunt Cleo who lived in Bellingham, near Catford. I remember cycling to her home one Sunday morning. Like Hubert and Persia, she remarked on my "Wheatle" looks. She offered me a delicious Jamaican dinner, and she talked about the Wheatle clans, especially in the Jamaican parish of Trelawney.

It was fascinating to learn about the various threads of the Wheatle family, but as the weeks and months rolled on, I began to feel a little disillusioned. *Where is my father in all this?* And I hadn't made any progress at all regarding my mother's side of the family. There were ten times more DaCostas in the phone book than Wheatles. I didn't even know where to start.

"You love your writing, right?" Aunt Cleo had asked me that first time I paid her a visit. "Why don't you write a letter to the Jamaican *Gleaner* newspaper or Radio Jamaica?"

"Can I do that?" I queried. "Will they print or broadcast it?"

"You won't know that answer till you try," she replied. "Write a letter!"

I hesitated. I didn't want the whole of Jamaica reading or hearing about my personal affairs. *What would I say in this letter? Would my parents even respond to it?*

I stayed focused on raising my children and on my work. I had accomplished so much. I had traced second, third, and fourth cousins, and I was more than happy establishing those relationships.

But the question mark about my parents that had parked in a back corridor of my mind refused to switch off its light.

I watched my children celebrate christenings and birthdays. Beverley's family was always in attendance. *Don't Marvin, Tyrone, and Serena deserve to know my parents? Aunts, uncles, and cousins?*

JAMAICAN RADIO
AND DRAGON STOUT

In the spring of 1986, I sat down at my dinner table and penned two letters. One was addressed to the Jamaican *Gleaner* and the other to Radio Jamaica.

Two months later, the *Gleaner* responded to my letter and informed me they were about to write an article about my search for my family and publish my letter. They requested a recent photograph of myself to accompany the piece.

Oh my God!

It was a huge moment. I asked the kind people at the *Gleaner* to send me a copy of the newspaper when the piece ran.

Is this really happening?

A few weeks following the publication of my article, dozens of letters were sent to me via the *Gleaner*. I eagerly opened them.

Every single correspondence was from a young Jamaican woman wanting to know if I was searching for a wife. They included recent photographs of themselves, and they promised to cook for me and look after me well if I could only sponsor their visa application. They empathized with the search for my family and promised that they would never allow me to suffer loneliness. Reading the handwritten notes did wonders for my ego, but Beverley wasn't impressed.

Radio Jamaica finally replied to my letter stating that on one of their scheduled programs, they had a slot that helped Jamaicans from overseas reconnect with their families on the island.

In August 1986, Radio Jamaica broadcast a thirty-second clip about my search for my parents.

My father Alfred was enjoying a cool Dragon Stout in a bar in Old Harbour when he heard the announcement. He almost choked on his favorite beer. When he overcame his initial shock, he penned a letter to me via Radio Jamaica, and it arrived through my letter box in mid-September 1986.

I read my father's words through disbelieving eyes. He apologized for not returning to England to claim me, but he had thought that I would be looked after very well. (How wrong he was.) He invited me to come over to Jamaica and visit, but before doing so, I should look for his sister Hermine, who still lived in Brixton.

I have an aunt who lives in Brixton? Are you fucking kidding me? Why wasn't I told this before?

I reread my social services files. I couldn't find any mention of a Hermine. Rage swelled in my chest. *This so-called father abandoned me, placed me in care, and didn't bother informing the social services that I have family living in Brixton. How fucking cruel is that?*

I controlled my fury enough to visit Hermine on Milkwood Road, Brixton (only five minutes up the street from the Lambeth social services area three office). I didn't know whether to skank with joy or to weep bitter tears.

Aunt Hermine herself opened the door and gazed at me for a long while. Her smile almost kissed the doorframe.

Tears ran down her cheeks. "Alfred cyan't deny you," she said. "You favor him. Come in! Come in!" She called out to her husband: "John! John! Come here! You never going to believe this!"

Uncle John came in from the garden and did a double take. "Freddy!" he said. "You favor your daddy!"

I wanted to jump around and scream. Jennifer Lara's "Jah Will Lead Us Home" played in my mind.

Uncle John led me to the front room and poured me a generous rum and Coke. "Yes, me know your daddy good," he said. "We cuss his backside becah we know he had ah son—"

"He wouldn't tell us where you deh," Aunt Hermine cut in. "But t'ank the lord! You have found us now."

For the rest of that Sunday afternoon, Aunt Hermine and Uncle John told me about things that my father loved doing: going to the dog track, wearing suits and skinny ties, listening to big bands, riding the bumper cars at the funfair, and so much more.

I was shown family pictures. There was one photograph of Aunt Hermine and Uncle John on their wedding day in the fall of 1962. My father was the best man. There he was in a dark suit, beaming at the photographer. It was taken a few weeks before my birth.

Anger soared in me once more, but I managed to control it.

There were other framed family photographs hanging from the walls, including one of my paternal grandparents' wedding way back in the early 1930s. My grandfather, Louis "Charlie" Wheatle, had been born in 1900. Family legend says he arrived in Old Harbour as a teenager, unwilling to speak about his family or where he came from.

Aunt Hermine searched for documents in her bedroom, and when she found what she was looking for, her grin stretched as wide as a Shaka double-bass speaker box. What she handed to me blew my mind.

PRIVATE AND CONFIDENTIAL

10 Downing Street
Whitehall
December 14, 1956.

Mr. Louis Wheatle,
    I have the honour to inform you that the Queen has been graciously pleased to approve the Prime Minister's recommendation that the Medal of the Order of the British Empire (B.E.M.) be awarded to you. Your name therefore appears in the List of Honours to be published on January 1.

I am, Sir,
Your obedient Servant

Aunt Hermine couldn't stop laughing as she passed me another official letter. "My fader won the award for long service to Bodles Agricultural Station inna Old Harbour," she explained. "Him start work there as a teenager way back in 1915."

PRIVATE AND CONFIDENTIAL

29th December, 1956

My dear Mr. Wheatle,
    This letter will probably not reach you before the an-

nouncement is made but I am very glad indeed to congratulate you on the fact that Her Majesty the Queen has awarded to you the British Empire Medal in the New Year's Honour List.

I am delighted that the excellent work which you have done over the past years has been recognised in this way.

I should add that the first announcement will be made over Radio Jamaica after the 9 o'clock news on New Year's Eve and the List of Honours will be published in the papers on the 2nd of January. Until the official announcement is made you should, of course, treat this as strictly confidential to yourself.

Yours sincerely,
Hugh Foot
Governor of Jamaica

I felt a surge of pride.

Aunt Hermine cried and hugged me.

"How is Granddad now?" I asked.

"He's quite sick," Aunt Hermine told me. "I'm going to see him next month. Can you come with me?"

"I don't have the money for the flight just yet," I replied. "I'll save up and go as soon as I can."

Louis Wheatle passed away before I could meet him. He never knew it, but he played a big part in me finding my identity. (Years later, I employed my grandfather's mysterious young adult life to build my *Island Songs* narrative.)

I was introduced to Aunt Hermine and Uncle John's children: Jackie, Gary, and Debbie. Aunt Hermine also had an older son, Junior, who had left home.

Later that night, I asked, "Did you know my mother?"

Aunt Hermine and Uncle John shared a knowing look.

"Of course me knew her," my aunt finally replied. "Alfred loved that girl! He was always chatting about her. She had beautiful long hair. Indian blood was in her. Pretty she was pretty! He called her Myna. Somebody told me she was married, and that Myna's husband was in Jamaica. Alfred never care."

"Me did warn him," Uncle John said. *"Don't get yourself involved wid another mon's wife.* But Alfred never listen to anybody."

"They were two grown people," Aunt Hermine said. "They knew what they were doing. The both of dem were responsible."

"There was all this bangarang and fuss," John added. "But you, the chile, shoulda come first. They shoulda work together to come up wid the best solution."

I started visiting Aunt Hermine and Uncle John every other Sunday. I introduced Beverley and my young children to them.

Uncle John would entertain me in the lounge with his video collection: he was a big fan of Clint Eastwood, Bruce Lee, and Sylvester Stallone. He also had an impressive record box of ska, rock steady, and reggae albums. "Al, do you have this?" He would grin as he played a 7" track from the likes of Alton Ellis, Desmond Dekker, Jimmy Cliff, the Heptones, Stranger Cole, or Toots and the Maytals.

I wrote to Alfred every month or so, sending him photographs of my children and bringing him up to date on family events. On one level, we bonded, but on another, I simply could not let go that this was the man who had abandoned me to a childhood hell. I wasn't sure if I had the goodness within me to ever forgive him.

"Listen to what him have to say," Simeon advised. "Give him ah chance. Don't do anyting foolish, Alex Wheatle."

"But he dumped me in care and didn't come back for me," I countered.

"Everybody mek mistakes," Simeon reasoned. "Including me. Some sufferahs in this world never get to know dem family. You have ah chance."

Although I couldn't offer Simeon any guarantees, I saved hard for my trip to Jamaica.

I decided to travel just before Christmas 1987.

PILGRIMAGE TO JAMAICA

In December 1987, a few weeks before my twenty-fifth birthday, I settled into my seat for my flight to Kingston. As the stewardess checked my seat belt, I still hadn't decided if I should embrace my father or kill him.

He had abandoned me to the Lambeth social services before I had reached the age of two. He returned to Jamaica soon afterward, deserting me to my fate in a brutal children's home. I had suffered physical, sexual, and mental abuse in my formative years. Bitterness and vengeance seared through my veins. It proved difficult to temper my emotions as Simeon had advised.

Since I had tracked him down, his letters had been understanding, repentant, and apologetic. I couldn't help but admire his handwriting skills. *Sincerely, your loving father,* he would sign them. He wrote that he was a woodwork and technical drawing teacher in a Kingston school. *Did he ever think about my education? What would he have made of my three school expulsions? Did he ever fret about how I was being cared for by my so-called guardians?*

That trip to Jamaica was my first. A cocktail of anxiety and foreboding almost made me throw up during takeoff. Unsure if I could keep it down, I politely declined lunch and any alcohol.

Taking breaks from reading Richard Wright's *Native Son*, I counted the hours down till our arrival. I cared little for the small talk of the passenger beside me.

A galaxy of lights that stretched out and climbed the dark sheer rises in the distance greeted our descent as we flew over Kingston Harbour. The warm Caribbean night hit me when I walked down the steps of the plane. Then I took my first stride on Jamaican soil. I had landed on the island of my heroes: Paul Bogle, Sam Sharpe, Queen Nanny, Miss Lou, Bob Marley, Burning Spear, Dennis Brown, Gregory Isaacs, Sugar Minott, King Yellowman, Marcia Griffiths, Sister Nancy, Johnny Osbourne, Lee "Scratch" Perry, Jimmy Cliff, Toots and the Maytals, King Tubby, Barrington Levy, Don Quarrie, Merlene Ottey, Michael Holding, and so many more. It was overwhelming. This was the final stop on my journey to reclaim my identity.

The heaving, boisterous throng waiting at the arrivals gate intimidated me. My father had warned me in his last letter not to trust the quick-fingered, sunglassed men who would offer to carry my luggage. *They will drive you somewhere, tek everything you have, and kill you.*

My uncle Lloyd found me at the airport. I felt a peculiar emotion as I studied this man who shared the same features as me. I would be staying with him for my first night in Jamaica before I drove out to where my father resided in Old Harbour.

Uncle Lloyd asked me if I'd had a good flight. I said yes. I didn't reveal that I had wrestled endlessly in my mind with whether or not I should kill my father. He grinned and slapped my shoulder when I presented him with a box of duty-free cigarettes. As we cruised along the strip of land that jutted out to the airport, I couldn't help but recall James Bond overcoming a Spectre assassin on this same track of tarmac in *Dr. No*. The Caribbean Sea gently frothed and twinkled in the moonlight on both sides of me.

My uncle lived in a bungalow, a goat walk away from the University of the West Indies's Mona campus, where his wife Lallice taught English. She served me a supper of ackee, salt-fish, yams, and green bananas. My belly full, I retired to bed early. The surrounding cicadas disturbed my toxic thoughts about my father.

I was awoken by a rooster chorus—they were answering each other in the surrounding hills. I had breakfast on the veranda, marveling at the vivid green around me and listening to the local news on a radio that was hooked on a rusty nail. I was introduced to my cousins Jonathan and Melanie who were excited to meet me. I could see the resemblance, which again freaked me out. Uncle Lloyd had another son, David, who lived in Montego Bay.

The sun shone as brightly as I had ever seen it. Folks passing by paused to say good morning. They commented on my Wheatle forehead and eyes. Children giggled at my English accent.

Uncle Lloyd decided to take me on a short tour of his neighborhood. He admitted that he'd never really gotten along with my father, and when he had learned that he'd abandoned his one and only son in a children's home, he went to his house to remonstrate with him. He explained to me that my father usually arrived home from school around five p.m., so we wouldn't leave for Old Harbour until around four. I couldn't hide my disappointment—I wanted to confront my father as soon as possible. My rage stirred within me.

"How do you feel?" Uncle Lloyd asked me.

"I don't know," I replied. "How would you feel if you were just about to meet the man who ditched you to a life of hell?"

"You sure you want to do this, Alex?"

"Yes," I nodded. Hot adrenaline rushed through my body and I clenched both fists. James Bond killing Professor Dent in a bamboo cottage high in the hills above Kingston came to mind. *Maybe I'll have to escape to a Crab Key–like island if I slay my own father.*

"I'll be all right," I lied.

Uncle Lloyd pulled on his cigarette and glanced at me suspiciously.

That morning was the longest of my life. After lunch we trekked uphill to Papine where the Rastafarians played their drums and recited passages from the Bible on a small strip of green in the middle of town. Vendors riding rust-bitten bikes sold sky juice, cola, and peanut punch to the watching crowd. Elderly residents sat on their stoops while others swept out their front yards. Electric cables, suspended from leaning telegraph poles, crisscrossed from one corrugated roof to another. In the gulleys, scrawny dogs snouted for scraps. The Blue Mountains rose regally in the distance. I was impressed by the neatness of the school uniforms the students wore. The reggae music booming out from cars, vans, and buses was a constant backdrop to every conversation and argument. At every turn and corner I heard the trending crop of Jamaican dancehall talent: Lieutenant Stitchie, Admiral Bailey, Professor Nuts, Major Mackerel, Pinchers, Leroy Gibbons, Half Pint, and Red Dragon. The rich flavors of the market teased my nostrils, and the traders were not shy in trying to secure a sale. I was even more amazed when Lloyd informed me that Bob Marley himself had regularly shopped for ital food in the Papine market. He promised me that once I had met my father, he would take me to my hero's former residence on Hope Road, only a few bus stops away.

We made a brief visit to my aunt Lilleth where she was staying in the former home of my grandfather Louis on Gordon Town Road. Sadly, Louis had lost his battle with cancer a few months earlier. He was buried in Dovecot Memorial Park where days later I paid my respects.

As Aunt Lilleth made us a generous lunch of ackee, fried dumplings, and saltfish, she criticized Alfred for abandoning me. "How could him do dat? Me will cuss his wort'less behind yesterday, today, and tomorrow for dat great tribulation! When you go and see him, tell your fader him cyan never mek it up to you. Tell him! That damn John Crow!"

"I will, Aunt Lilleth."

"Mek sure you do. And if him give you any excuse, tell him me will tek de next bus up to Old Harbour and cuss him till him ears crackle, blister, and drop off!"

"I'll try."

"That damn Alfred!" Aunt Lilleth continued. "Also, tell him dat wearing dat damn baseball cap don't mek him look younger. We all know him bald like ah black pumpkin. Tell him dat!"

Aunt Lilleth had once lived in Brixton but decided to leave after a white man spat on her at a bus stop on Clapham Road. With her husband Neville, she emigrated to Toronto, Canada. Every summer and Christmas, she flew back to Jamaica to visit family.

Readers of my novel *Island Songs* have praised the colorful patois dialogue in the text. Truth is, it was inspired by Aunt Lilleth's wit, originality, and vocal delivery.

FINAL DESTINATION

....

We finally set off for Old Harbour just after four. My heart-beat accelerated.

The Half Way Tree junction was snarled with traffic. The thick exhaust fumes blended into the hazy horizon. Bare-footed kids weaved in and out of the traffic selling a wide variety of nuts and berries. The tooting and honking was like an Olympic sport. Pedestrians, taking their time in the fierce sun, were harassed from all sides. We drove on toward Spanish Town, the old conquistador capital of Jamaica. Uncle Lloyd pointed out the rum distilleries on the way.

Skinny goats plodded along even skinnier sidewalks. Bare-backed vendors shoved their wooden carts along on crooked wheels. Sugarcane fields suddenly appeared. My memory decided to play a reel of my most violent episodes in the children's home—beaten with fire pokers, wooden hair brushes, leather straps, steel ladles, and hard shoes. I asked my eternal questions: *Where are my parents? Do I truly belong to any family out there in the wide world? Will they make me feel welcome? Will they offer a good reason for why they abandoned me? Have they carried me in their thoughts for my twenty-four years?*

I checked a road sign: *Old Harbour, 4 miles.* The fury

within me soared. Uncle Lloyd stopped off at a bar where he bought me a Red Stripe. The sun blazed down and the sensation of the drink hitting the back of my throat was pleasant.

My uncle searched my eyes once more. "Are you sure you're up for this?"

I thought about it for a few seconds. "Yes, I at least have to know why he left me."

We climbed back into the car. Soon, we turned right at a water tower, half a mile before the center of Old Harbour. Goats could have hidden in the potholes. The road climbed, twisted, and swerved. The once-bright sun had now turned amber—it hovered over the western hills. The cicadas and grasshoppers had come out to play. The view over St. Catherine was spectacular. I could just about see the Caribbean Sea. I wondered in what direction Sligoville was located, the town where Simeon ran away to and joined a Rastafarian commune.

Uncle Lloyd pulled up outside a bungalow that was painted cream and sky-blue. It was fronted by a small but neat lawn where an almond tree rose splendidly in the middle, its white-pinkish leaves reflecting the sunset. Whitewashed rocks stood outside the shoulder-high gate. To calm my nerves, I lit one of my uncle's cigarettes as he stepped out of the car. I sucked on it hard and wished it was a spliff. Uncle Lloyd rat-a-tatted his keys against the gate and the front door opened. I jumped out of my seat. A tall man appeared. He was wearing a red baseball cap and square-shaped glasses. A checked shirt hung loose on his lean frame. His beard was flecked with coarse wires of gray. His complexion was darker than mine but there was no escaping the resemblance: he had the same forehead and dark eyes. I was thinking he could have at least bestowed his height on me.

"Lloyd," he called, "you have Al with you?"
"Yes," Lloyd replied, "see him there."

My father and me posing in his garden in Old Harbour, Jamaica, 1987

My father came forward, stopped by the gate, and studied me. I couldn't meet his gaze. Instead, I looked at the white rocks. In my mind's eye I could see him prostrate on his own lawn, blood seeping from his forehead.

He opened the gate and unease marked his face. "Lloyd," he called, "are you staying? You want a rum or something?"

"No, man," my uncle replied. "You two have nuff to talk

about." He lifted my overnight bag from the car boot and handed it to me, then climbed back into the driver's seat, lit a cigarette, and started the engine. "If you want, I will come for you later," he said.

He pulled away, leaving my father and me alone. A red sun dipped beyond the western ranges. The cicadas seemed to scream louder. My father invited me to take a seat on his veranda. Tiny red ants crawled over the concrete. A skinny lizard stopped to take a look before scurrying on its way.

"I have beer in the fridge, or if you want, I have some rum and Coke?"

"I'll have a rum and Coke," I said.

He grabbed my bag and was gone for ten minutes. It shouldn't have taken that long just to fetch drinks. Maybe he sensed the peril he was in.

I stood up and examined the house—my father had built it himself. I was impressed. *If he could do this, why didn't he stay in England?*

Alfred returned with my refreshment and a Dragon Stout for himself. *Maybe after I drink this, I'll lick him on the head with the glass!*

Alfred raised his bottle, but I rejected his toast. I took a swig, leaned forward, and eye-drilled him. "Why?"

He avoided my vicious glare and took a long glug of his beer. "It . . . it was hard for a man to look after a small child in England in those days. The pressure got to me."

Instantly, I thought of "Pressure Drop" by Toots and the Maytals. That's how my mind works. "The pressure got to you? What about the pressure I had to live with for so many years? Living in that home! When I was a kid, they beat me up almost every day. What about that? You wouldn't believe what they put me through."

"But Al . . ." My father tried to find words.

I couldn't look at him. Undiluted anger fizzed and burned inside of me. I stood up and walked to the front gate. The white rocks grew large in my eyes. I gazed at one in particular. *I could lick him with it. Crack his skull with it.* I opened the gate.

"It wouldn't take much for you to be a better father to your children than I was to you," he called out. "How are they? How is little Serena? She's two and a half now, isn't she?"

I closed my eyes and thought of my young family back home in London. I could almost feel Serena riding on my shoulders in our lounge as we chased Marvin and Tyrone. We would dodge the furniture and pull up short of the walls. I carried their laughter and thrills with me. Alfred had never known that joy with me.

"Al, how is your family? Do you have a recent picture?"

I closed the gate and rejoined Alfred. "They're fine. They tire Bev and me out but we wouldn't have it any other way."

He nodded and sipped his drink, then offered me a plastic smile. I found myself pitying him and drew in a long breath. The tension in my limbs relaxed. I asked for another drink. *Maybe I should get to know this man. Many of the friends I grew up with will never have this opportunity. Alex, give it a go.*

"You like cricket, don't you?" Alfred asked.

"Love it," I said.

"So what do you think of the current West Indies team?"

"I love Viv Richards, the master blaster. He's my hero. The bowler pitches the ball too short and he smashes it to the boundary!"

Alfred laughed loud and the tension drained from his face.

We talked cricket and politics into the night.

CORRUGATED JUNGLE

....

The next morning, Alfred invited me to take a trip to downtown Kingston. He was very quiet over breakfast. All he said to me was, "Al, me understand why you're so vex, but it could have been worse."

I didn't respond. "Where are you taking me?" I asked.

"You'll see."

We caught a bus to Half Way Tree, Kingston, before taking another along Orange Street to downtown. We stepped off the coach only to be greeted by a cloud of black exhaust fumes.

Hustle and bustle surrounded me. Every other vehicle tooted its horn. Vendors pushed their carts on wonky wheels. Jamaican curses split the hot air. The sun seemed to blaze down harder in this corner of Kingston. Sweat dripped off me. Alfred had a flannel banked in his back pocket; I should have carried one too.

We made our way to Coronation Market where Alfred bought yams, coconuts, green beans, breadfruit, and sweet potatoes. The higgler wrapped the vegetables in black plastic bags. We walked through to Tivoli Gardens, a poor residential area where corrugated iron sheets were the primary roofing material, and a single standpipe in the street seemed to be the main water source. There were no proper sidewalks. Open bags of rubbish collected in corners and piled high against walls. I sensed the salty aroma of the sea.

Barefoot children played and ran through the narrow lanes that separated blocks of dwellings. Sometimes they stood still and stared at us before scampering on. Their raggedy T-shirts and shorts clung to them. Their calves and feet were the same color as the dirt tracks they raced on. Jimmy London's "It Ain't Easy" played in my mind: *Living in a ghetto in a tenement yard, it ain't easy . . .*

This is reality, Alex. Not a song in your mind.

We hit Spanish Town Road. On our left, toward the sea, stood the May Pen Cemetery.

Alfred pressed on, occasionally swabbing his forehead with his flannel. He smoked a cigarette every ten minutes or so. He was fifty-four years old—I could only admire his fortitude walking in that intense heat.

The dilapidated Trench Town residences came into view. It was difficult to see where one home began and another ended. Cheap corrugated roofing sheets lined the dusty streets along with slats of wood and chipboard. The occasional breeze-block wall interrupted the DIY patchwork, as did Rastafarian splashes of red, gold, and green. I could smell the chicken claw, pumpkin, and vegetable soup from outdoor kitchens.

Overhead cables and wires hung precariously from leaning telegraph poles. I couldn't help thinking that if a single bird decided to perch on any line, the whole community might tumble down on itself.

Alfred bought two boxes of sky juice from a vendor. It wasn't quite to my taste but I downed half of it in one gulp.

"Tek time, mon," Alfred said. "Tek time!"

We trod on close to Fifth Street. Alfred pointed out the bullet-ridden buildings and walls where political gangs fought running battles. He didn't need to add a commentary. Indeed, things could have been worse for me.

We headed out of Trench Town and made a pilgrimage to Maxfield Avenue in West Kingston. I wanted to stand outside the legendary Channel One recording studio.

Built by the Chinese-Jamaican Hoo Kim brothers in 1972, Channel One had produced a fair portion of the greatest reggae records in history. The house band, the Revolutionaries, included in my opinion the ultimate rhythm section in the ace drummer Lowell "Sly" Dunbar and the late, great bassist Robbie Shakespeare. They also had Tommy McCook, a founding member of the Skatalites, on tenor saxophone. Tommy had once been a resident at the Alpha Boys School orphanage which was administered by nuns. He was introduced to playing musical instruments there.

Painted on the front wall of the Channel One complex was an image of a vinyl record beside the number *1*. It didn't look anything like the zebra crossing close to the famous Abbey Road Studios in a leafy corner of North London. It was difficult to comprehend that I stood outside the walls where the Mighty Diamonds had recorded their *Right Time* album, and so many other reggae artists had voiced their own classics.

My only regret was that Alfred had warned me not to bring my camera for my trip downtown. "That will mark you out," he had said. "You don't want to bring any attention to yourself. Badmon and robbermon all about."

"Do you know where King Tubby's quarter tower is?" I asked.

"Me don't know," he replied. "Maybe that trip will be for another day."

We returned to Coronation Market and caught a bus back to Half Way Tree. There, we visited Devon House, where I treated Alfred to a chocolate ice cream and enjoyed the lush grounds and took shelter from the fierce sun.

It was a good day.

At the end of it, I thought about those poor children playing in the dusty streets of Tivoli Gardens and Trench Town. *What life opportunities do they have? What will they be eating tonight? Where will they be sleeping tonight? I doubt they have ever enjoyed a scoop of ice cream at Devon House. Who am I to complain about the life opportunities presented to me?*

I thanked the Most High for the blessings I had. From this point onward, I tried not to think of myself as a victim.

Simeon had always encouraged me to read and learn about the world's religions. "Religion? Mek up your own mind," he advised. "Me nuh here to convert yuh to anyting."

I read passages of the Bible and the Koran. In my conclusion, Christianity and Islam each owned a history of conquest, brutality, and forced conversion. I found the rules, sacrifices, and rituals too demanding. I could never understand why a man or woman who chose celibacy was placed on a higher plane of respect and deference. I couldn't comprehend why the leaders of faiths built themselves huge palaces and decorated them with priceless art.

In Matthew 19:21, Jesus says to a man, *If you want to be perfect, go, sell your possessions and give to the poor, and you will have treasure in heaven. Then come, follow me.* I fail to see any leader of the world's religions acting on this.

Rasta bredren at the Twelve Tribes of Israel in Kennington, South London, repeated to me that Haile Selassie was the King of Kings and the Lord of Lords. "Direct descendant from King Solomon and the Queen of Sheba!" they claimed.

I reasoned that King Solomon had many wives and concubines who gave birth to hundreds if not thousands of his children. I pointed out that it was likely that many people now living in the Middle East were descendants of King Solomon.

What attracted to me to Rastafari was that it offered me an identity. I no longer looked for a European-looking white guy with flowing shampooed hair and an immaculate white robe as my deity.

Simeon schooled me that the Roman emperor Constantine and his council of Nicaea edited the Bible in 325 AD. "Alex, do you really think they're going to select the books that fill the Bible for the benefit of the Black mon or woman? No sah. And they're doing the same ting today. Why do you think rich people want to control the newspapers and media?"

"Why?" I asked.

"To control what people think and believe," Simeon responded. "Dat's how Babylon work."

I once asked a priest how a young child who died from starvation could be condemned to an afterlife in hell because he or she wasn't raised in the Christian faith. The man of God struggled for an answer.

If a religion failed to cater to the sufferahs in the world and refused to accept the circumstances of their birth or the faith they were raised in, it wasn't for me.

Returning to my father's home following my trip to downtown Kingston, my mind could not rid itself of the images I had seen that day.

Is there a God?

I like to think so, but this doesn't mean it has to be Christian, Muslim, or any other recognized divinity.

DANGEROUS DRIVING

....

The next morning, Aunt Lilleth arrived outside Alfred's home in a taxi to kidnap me.

"Alfred," Aunt Lilleth called from her ride, "are you just going to chat pure foolishness in Al's ears de whole morning time? Me come to show Al Jamaica. He needs to see the North Coast and how beautiful the sea is."

"But me taking Al to Port Royal tomorrow," Alfred protested. "He can see the sea there."

"Dat is tomorrow," Aunt Lilleth said. "And there is no beach at Port Royal. Al cyan't swim there. What about today?"

"I was going to take him to a craft market."

"Craft market? And let dem vendor women hustle and hassle him? No sah! Me nuh want me good nephew to buck up on any vendor trickster. It'll be like taking ah blood sample to ah vampire party."

Aunt Lilleth suggested I pack a towel and swimming trunks.

Soon, we drove across the country to the North Coast. As we twisted and weaved through narrow high passes and skirted sheer drops, I suffered heart seizure ten times and died five. When I wasn't offering my last prayers, I took in the rich green scenery all around me. It was truly wonderful, especially whenever we passed a small village where there was always a beautifully kept, brightly painted church. When I glanced upward, it was hard to imagine how families squeezed into their tiny shanty dwellings that clung for sweet life onto steep hillsides.

With much relief, we arrived in Puerto Seco, Discovery Bay. The first port of call was a beach bar where I bought everyone a drink. Truth was, I was trying to rebuild my crumbled nerves.

There was no denying the call of the Caribbean. It was an altogether different shade of blue than what Bognor Regis offered. I swam for half an hour or so before I sat on the beach with Aunt Lilleth. Our taxi driver, Roy, went off to look for herb.

"I will never forgive Alfred," Lilleth told me. "But you is family now. Hermine and meself now look 'pon you like ah son. Never forget that, Al. You're not alone. You should have never been alone."

I did my very best not to weep.

Roy bought enough weed for two spliffs. As I lit mine, Aunt Lilleth peered into the horizon. Maybe she guessed that I needed to be well charged for the return journey. I wasn't sure if my vital organs could endure the death ride along the high mountain passes again.

Aunt Lilleth did not return me to Alfred the next day. Instead, she introduced me to my uncle Floyd, who lived and worked at the Bodles Agricultural Complex between Old Harbour and Maypen. He and his wife Amy had five children: Tony, Ashley, Chris, Debbie, and Kadeen. Their small home was surrounded by mango trees. From one of the tree's branches, a tire was suspended from a rope.

My father and Aunt Lilleth in the UK, 1962

Uncle Floyd was responsible for the maintenance of the water pumphouse that served the surrounding fields. He rose at three thirty six mornings a week; he had taken over the duties of my grandfather who had worked there for nigh on sixty years.

It was a peaceful day, offering me space to reset my life goals.

As darkness fell, Amy served the family fish and rice. Nightlife, a friend of the family, shared his homegrown weed. The banter, like in many Jamaican families, was raucous and animated. The Red Stripe beer and white rum flowed. The sense of belonging was so overwhelming that at one point during the evening, I wept openly. Nightlife wrapped me another spliff. "Nuh worry yaself, Al," he said. "You're wid family now. You're wid blood. Tek ah lick."

Eventually, Alfred did bring me to Port Royal, which was far more fascinating than I had imagined. The narrative of the "wickedest city on earth" being destroyed by an earthquake was biblical.

I discovered that in the seventeenth century, Port Royal was the world's most notorious pirate hub, where fortunes and lives could be made and lost. I learned about the deeds of Calico Jack, Blackbeard, Captain Morgan, Mary Read, and Anne Bonny. It must have planted a seed, because thirty-five years later I penned my second historical novel, *Kemosha of the Caribbean*, which is set largely in seventeenth-century Port Royal.

I steeled myself for another death ride on a pilgrimage to Nine Miles, St. Ann, the birthplace of Bob Marley. Alfred excused himself from the trip, but Aunt Lilleth was more than willing. "The breadfruit and jackfruit cheaper inna country," she said.

What first struck me was the stunning scenery. I was surrounded by endless lush green. A gentle breeze disturbed the treetops, and the birds didn't seem to flap their wings, they simply glided with minimal effort.

The hilltop homes and huts were basic. Locals walked a bit slower than their cousins in the city. There were no shiny buildings, shops with fancy facades, or long buses snarled in traffic like in downtown Kingston. It was a place where women still carried their groceries on their heads, and where goats navigated paths up sheer rises.

I could write a novel with this setting, I said to myself.

Indeed, I did. *Island Songs* was eventually published in 2005 and is full of this countryside. In my opinion, it's my greatest literary achievement to date.

To stand close to Bob Marley's tomb was and still is indescribable. So many emotions flowed through me. I was reminded of both the fragility and preciousness of life. I recalled my constant battles with my ultimate enemy, loneliness. I had to accept that it would always be with me; I'll take my emotional scars to the grave.

My stomach remembered my bouts of hunger in Elm Park. I thought of Simeon and the life lessons he taught me in prison. I reflected on my childhood in Holly House, Shirley Oaks, and praying at night for a family to claim me. I recollected the moment when Valentine first introduced me to reggae. *Skanga, skanga, skanga.* I thought of the East Croydon YMCA disco where the DJ played Junior Murvin's "Police & Thieves." I fondly reminisced about building my first bass speaker box in Valentine's back garden. I prayed that my mother, who I had yet to trace and be reunited with, was still alive. It all led me to standing perfectly still outside Bob Marley's vault.

"Everybody has a purpose" was one of Simeon's mantras. "You have to work out which purpose is yours becah it don't always just drop into your lap."

Whatever talent I have, I must not waste it, I told myself, then closed my eyes and softly sang my favorite Bob Marley song: *There's a natural mystic blowing in the air. If you listen carefully now, you will hear . . .*

As I relaxed into my British Airways flight for my return to London, I vowed that if I was ever granted the opportunity to establish myself in songwriting, poetry, fiction, or indeed any of the arts, I would take the lead of my favorite reggae artists. I'd express my lived experiences and those of my fellow sufferahs. I would be a living witness to their stories. I would take them out of the shadows and make them visible. *What about the half that's never been told?* sang Dennis Brown. I desperately wanted to give voice to that half.

AFTERWORD

WORKING MY TALENT

....

For the next ten years I nurtured my relationship with my father. I'd fly out to Jamaica every other year and stay at his bungalow in Old Harbour. Our safe talking ground was politics and cricket. We'd end up arguing if we discussed anything else. He introduced me to many of his friends who lived in Old Harbour and beyond. "This is my son, you know. He's going to be a big-time writer one day!"

I flew to Toronto, Canada, where I was reunited with Aunt Lilleth. She introduced me to her sister Kathleen and the rest of the Wheatle clan in her part of the world. I now had more relatives than I could count. It was bewildering.

I continued my career in engineering, making components for aircraft.

Beverley and I moved to a new flat in Clapham Junction, South London. The local council had discovered that our old block on Nine Elms Lane was riddled with asbestos—the building was condemned.

We held birthday parties for our growing children. It was a joy for me to watch their excited faces as relatives and friends arrived at our home armed with cards, presents, smiles, and warm hugs. Marvin had a gift for art, Tyrone the ability to charm anyone with his wit and humor, and Serena excelled in school.

I signed up for creative writing seminars and workshops. I attended readings in libraries and bookstores. I was inspired by Ray Shell's novel *Iced,* which was written from a Black perspective. New Black British writers emerged. Patrick Augustus penned the Baby Father series. Naomi King published *O.P.P. (Other People's Property)* which was a massive underground hit. Vanessa Walters, a teenage prodigy, had *Rude Girls* gracing the bookshelves at just seventeen years old. Karline Smith published one of the best British urban novels ever committed to print, *Moss Side Massive.* Courttia Newland's *The Scholar* was released to great critical acclaim in 1997. As I tweaked and refined *Brixton Rock,* I knew my dream of being published was possible.

In the fall of 1997, I sat in the audience under the arches close to the Brixton train station where Sister Claudette Douglas, a spoken word artist and performance advocate, had launched her "Word" events. She had painted the brick walls orange and decorated them with African and Caribbean art from local artists. She had built a small stage where a performer could opt for a percussionist if they wished. She even provided a small bar at the rear of the space. The audience sipped their juices and mineral waters.

My heartbeat accelerated as I sat there holding my A4 notebook. Every now and again, a train rumbled overhead. I was due onstage next. My nerves jangled. There was no skanking crowd to provide a shield. No music. Just you, the stage, and the seated audience. It would have been so much easier if I'd had a mic in my hand and a rockers soundtrack to accompany me.

The thick notepad that I held formed the basis of my first

three novels: *Brixton Rock, East of Acre Lane,* and *The Seven Sisters* (later retitled *Home Boys).*

As I waited nervously for my name to be called, I reflected on my life journey. At twelve years of age, I stood up to Miss Joyce Cook who was about to beat me yet again. I'll never forget the look on her face when I punched her just above her right cheek, smashing her glasses. The state of terror that I had lived with up to that point rebounded onto her and she never physically troubled me again.

I remembered Brixtonians informing me about seventeen-year-old Olive Morris standing up to the police and intervening when she witnessed a Black brother being assaulted.

I flinched when my mind brought up the hollering and wailing from the cell next door to mine as Trevor suffered his beating.

There was the Day of Action march following the New Cross fire tragedy. I was proud that I had joined my fellow protesters on March 2, 1981. Five or so weeks later, I played an active role in the Brixton uprising. I do not regret my actions on that day, and still believe that brute force perpetrated by an oppressor must be met by an equal power to help change the aggressor's mindset.

Following the Brixton uprising, Black activists, leaders, and politicians began to fill spaces that had previously been occupied exclusively by white people. I remember watching the future Labour MP Paul Boateng with his big Afro, debating with a presenter on BBC's flagship *Newsnight* program. Boateng was discussing the plight of the urban sufferahs and how they were being brutalized by the police. The *Voice* newspaper was launched a year later. Black journalists were writing their articles from a Black British perspective. Onyekachi Wambu became my favorite columnist.

Even so, the Brixton uprising failed to truly correct the racism embedded in British institutions, and this included our interactions with the justice system, educational establishments, and places of employment.

In the early 1990s, I worked for an engineering firm in Park Royal, West London, that supplied components for military aircraft. I operated a CNC (computer numerical control) lathe machine. The white colleague who set the machine opposite me wrote, *I don't mind being called a nigger*, in a black marker on my backpack before I left for home one evening. The next morning, I marched into the company's boardroom where the managers were being briefed by the directors, threw my rucksack on the mahogany table, and said, "I ain't doing shit till you deal with this KKK fuckery!"

They were all white.

I was reprimanded for disrupting an important work meeting, given a warning, and ordered out of the boardroom. I made for the canteen where I sipped endless hot chocolates and read the morning papers. I refused to start my machine.

"Alex, they might sack you," a coworker warned me.

"I don't give a fuck," I spat back.

Later, the racist was warned about his future conduct after he claimed, "It was meant as a joke. Rappers are always using the N-word. Why doesn't Alex moan about that? Tell him I'll buy him a drink after work."

Only a small win, but for me it was important to lay down a marker that I wouldn't tolerate racism.

I never went for that drink.

Simeon once told me that it's easier to assimilate into a racist society and accept its trappings and rewards if you ignore the bigotry and disparity and never challenge white people's inherited and learned feelings of superiority. "They

238

will love you for that and accept you as one of dem!" Simeon growled.

By then living in Jamaica, Simeon was proud to receive my debut novel, *Brixton Rock*, when it was published in 1999. He sent me a ten-page critique saying I should have given more space to the Jah Nelson character and offered additional context for the motivations of my antagonist, Terry Flynn. *But for a first novel, you done good,* Simeon wrote. *Your potential is limitless. Don't let this novel be your last!*

Alfred built a small book stand in his front room and placed my novel on it where no visitor could fail to see it.

As the twentieth century closed, I exhausted all avenues trying to trace my mother, Almira. I didn't know what else I could do. I tried to keep this frustration in the back of my mind. At night, her specter would call in my dreams.

In 2000, following a witness statement that I provided for the prosecution for a trial concerning the pedophile William Hook, I agreed to meet with a counselor. I had two awkward sessions; I just didn't feel comfortable sharing my trauma and life experiences with a stranger.

As the new century reached three, four, five, six years old, it was difficult for me to accept that I might never know my mother or my siblings.

Despite Simeon warning me about receiving "tainted gongs from Babylon," in 2008 I accepted an M.B.E. (Member of the British Empire) from the queen. It was an award that was recommended by the government of the day, recognizing my significant contributions to British literature. I went to Buckingham Palace with Beverley, Aunt Hermine, and Beverley's aunt Cissy to receive it. In some quarters, I was branded a sellout. Simeon refused to correspond with me for a year.

I must admit that I struggled with accepting the award once I was notified. Like many others, I had a problem with the "empire" tag; it was difficult to ignore. One of the poets who I greatly admire, Benjamin Zephaniah, had publicly refused a similar honor.

In the end, I reasoned that someone out there had recognized the good I had done. That was quite something for me. My whole young life had been filled with authorities informing me that I was *nothing*. That I'd never achieve anything. They labeled me maladjusted. They said I was lucky to be cared for and so fortunate that the state had granted me food and shelter. When I left Shirley Oaks for the final time, they told me that I had already set my course for a life of delinquency and crime. They said I'd probably be dead before I reached the age of twenty-five.

What tipped me into acceptance was my cricketing idol, the great Sir Vivian Richards. The master blaster had refused to go on any West Indian cricket tours to South Africa from 1982 to 1984. If he had, I believe that decision would have destroyed West Indian cricket. He could have his fortune, but he stood firm. I remember him as fondly for that decision as much as his unequalled stroke play.

Then, in 1999, Viv Richards accepted a knighthood. Did that diminish his achievements?

Not at all.

He will forever be a hero of mine.

Family and close friends will tell you that I can be confrontational, combative, stubborn, headstrong, thin-skinned, and more. They might also tell you that I can be incredibly determined, loyal, compassionate, kind, and generous.

Simeon once schooled me about my early life: "Your starting blocks were way behind the line in the race of life. And when you finally catch up with some of your competitors, some will not like it. If you pass them, they will resent you. Some may even try to eliminate you." I knew he was quoting Bob Marley's "Who the Cap Fit."

"Beware of them negative people, Alex," Simeon went on. "Don't waste your energy on them. Some will smile at you and congratulate you. But behind your back they will slander and susu 'pon you. Just remember, you were born ah sufferah."

As always, Simeon's words manifested.

In more recent times, I've had various issues with the formation of the Black Writers' Guild. It had been established as a support network in the aftermath of George Floyd's murder. The primary goals were to represent Black UK writers in the publishing industry and lobby for equality.

My chief concern before joining was that a Black publisher seemed to have far more involvement and influence over decision-making and policy for the group than the vast majority of its members. For an organization that was supposedly set up for Black writers, I found this aspect problematic; I believed there was a conflict of interest.

A Zoom meeting was arranged where writers could also share their perspectives with the Black Writers' Guild leadership. After I expressed my uneasiness in a reasonable manner, I was told by the hierarchy that if I refused to become a member, any concerns I had didn't mean shit.

Oh well, I thought, *even if I'm a minority of one, I will forever stand my ground.*

I believe that Black people who have been offered platforms in the media, whether in publishing, television, radio, film, or any other medium, should be respectful and appreciate that the spaces they now occupy have been won through the spillage of Black blood in police cells, the loss of life, and the activism of the sufferahs who came before us and took to the streets.

I once complained to friends that despite winning several literary awards and being short-listed and nominated for many more, I had never been invited to become a member of the Royal Society of Literature or any other similar group for writers.

I knew why.

"Ah so it go," Simeon once said to me. "They're not your tribe and never will be. You write for the approval of the sufferah, not for those who look down on you. Don't look for validation from the people who hold you down." He selected an album from his Bob Marley collection and played a track to prove a point: "Get Up, Stand Up." The first two lines to this classic are in my opinion the greatest in protest song history:

Preacher man don't tell me
Heaven is under the earth . . .

It is claimed that Bob Marley wrote the opening verses of the song following a short trip to Haiti. He was shaken by the desperate poverty he witnessed. That is quite a statement when you consider that Marley himself suffered wretched hardship. He returned to Jamaica and fellow Wailer Peter Tosh finished the song with him:

You can fool some people sometimes
But you can't fool all the people all the time . . .

* * *

Me and Linton Kwesi Johnson at the Brixton Rock *book launch, 1999*

I am far from perfect, but I have tried to employ the gifts that the gods and ancestors bestowed on me at birth. I continually question myself: *Have you made sufferahs visible, Alex? Have you represented them?*

In the recesses of my mind, I have long hoped that wherever she is, my mother would be proud of me. If I ever stood in front of her, I wouldn't want her to be ashamed of me.

Starting in the late 1970s, the sufferah's voice began to be heard in the UK. British reggae bands including Dennis Bovell's Matumbi and Brinsley Forde's Aswad started to be played on the radio. *Babylon*, a film about the life of a sound system DJ/toaster, was released in 1980. Janet Kay, a lovers' rock singer, topped the national pop parade with "Silly Games." The dub poet Linton Kwesi Johnson not only played to sufferahs but a growing white liberal audience too. As we entered the late 1980s and early 1990s, sound system mic men like Maxi Priest, Tippa Irie, Smiley Culture, and Pato Banton began to enter the pop charts and even appeared on *Top of the Pops.*

I wanted to play my part in this new wave, to bring the sufferah's voice to the pages of fiction.

These developments filled my mind as I read an excerpt from my novel-in-progress, *Brixton Rock,* at Sister Claudette's "Word" event in 1997. The response was warm and encouraging. I left the stage believing I had launched a new career.

Valentine passed away in May 2001.

Simeon went to his reward in 2014.

When I bless my eyes on them again, they may recognize my flaws and my bad choices, but hopefully they will acknowledge that I have helped to make the invisible visible, and I have exhausted the gifts granted to me at birth.

"Don't allow the circumstances of your birth to dictate the rest of your life, Alex," Simeon kept repeating to me in our cell. "No sah. Sufferah have to shake off him tribulation and step forward."

ACKNOWLEDGMENTS

I always think of George Faith's "To Be a Lover," produced by the genius Lee "Scratch" Perry, when I'm blessed by kindness. There are a lot of compassionate, selfless people out there. In a time of greed, wealth disparity, and lack of compassion for others, we should never forget this.

My gratitude to the social worker Ms. C.A. Jarrold, who took me on a day trip to a farm when I was a child. It was only one afternoon, but for the first time that I can remember, I experienced the joys of childhood, discovery, and imagination. *There was another way.*

Eternal thanks to all the staff at St. Giles School (the Featherbed Lane site). Before I came under St. Giles's care, I never knew how a child was meant to be cared for, nurtured, and encouraged. You taught me empathy for others and recognized that I loved reading books. You found me a copy of *Treasure Island* that I brought home. At night I read it under my covers with a bicycle light. I closed my eyes and imagined I was sailing the high seas with Jim Hawkins and Long John Silver. I rode the waves on the *Hispaniola*. You urged me to express myself in art and crafts, and for the short time I spent with you, you were the only adults I trusted.

Thank you to Mr. Fred Dawes, who played football with

distinction for the Crystal Palace football club between 1936 and 1950, and went on to manage the team. You sparked my imagination whenever you shared your memories of being a child and loving the "beautiful game." I still remember you relating the "white horse" Wembley Cup final of 1923 and the wee Scottish forwards who thrashed England 5–1 in 1928. A broad smile twitched your cheeks as you retold the story of how the Magnificent Magyars, Hungary's talented team, embarrassed England by beating them 6–3 at Wembley Stadium in 1953. I fondly remember your tales of the great footballers of your day, including Stanley Matthews, Alex James, Nat Lofthouse, Tom Finney, Raich Carter, Tommy Lawton, Billy Wright, Ferenc Puskás, Alfredo Di Stéfano, Dixie Dean, the Black Pearl Eusébio, the flying Spanish winger Gento, and of course the incomparable Pelé. Fred, the owner of a newsagents on Wickham Road, Shirley, took pity on me as I flicked through the magazines I wanted to buy but couldn't afford. He offered me a paper round when I was eleven years old even though he didn't have to. A few shops on Wickham Road wouldn't even allow Shirley Oaks kids inside.

Big thanks to Valentine Golding's family: his mother and two sisters, Beryl and Jackie. You always shared your dinner with me and introduced me to the delights of West Indian food. Mrs. Golding's soup, complete with yams, dasheens, green bananas, and mutton, was a favorite.

Deepest thanks to Ms. Joyce Smith, one of my Shirley Oaks sisters, who always seemed to find something to cook in Elm Park when I was hungry. Your fried dumplings will forever remain unchallenged.

Big appreciation goes out to another Shirley Oaks sister, Jackie Fearon-Doyle, who resided in a children's home on St. Saviours Road, near Elm Park. Whenever the pantry was empty at Elm Park (quite often), I'd make the short trip to Jackie's at night, and she would raid her larder to give me what she could.

I can never repay my debt to my mentor and teacher, Simeon. If only we could clone you so any troubled teenager could listen and learn from your wise words and counsel. As long as I breathe, I'll tell the half that's never been told.

Thank you to Vanessa Walters, a friend of over twenty-five years, for her brilliant introduction to this volume. You're one of the best writers the UK has ever produced.

I have always been blessed enough to stumble upon kindness, and there have been many examples of this throughout my life. Massive thanks to anybody else who has supported me on my journey. I certainly wouldn't be here if empathy and love failed to touch me. This is why I refuse to see myself as a victim. Of course, I've experienced days where the only end I could see was me being dead. My life is living proof that once a sufferah receives the right care, understanding, kindness, and belief in their ability, they can achieve anything.

I have no long sermon to preach to anyone about how they should live their life. All I ask is to just have a little mercy for the sufferahs among us. That's all.

Lastly, thanks to my family: my wife Beverley and my children Marvin, Tyrone, and Serena. You have suffered my breakdowns, traumas, mood swings, outbursts, depressions, joys, successes, and highs right along with me. Everything I have is yours.

One Love,
Alex "Brixtonbard" Wheatle